FDR and High Treason
at Pearl Harbor

FDR and High Treason at Pearl Harbor

Roosevelt's Scandal

Charles P. Sprinkles
and
Nhan Thanh Thi Nguyen Sprinkles

Pen & Sword
MILITARY
AN IMPRINT OF PEN & SWORD BOOKS LTD.
YORKSHIRE - PHILADELPHIA

First published in Great Britain in 2023
by Pen & Sword Military
An imprint of
Pen & Sword Books Limited
Yorkshire - Philadelphia

Copyright © Charles Sprinkles and
Nhan Thanh Thi Nguyen Sprinkles, 2023

ISBN 978 1 39905 087 6

The right of Charles Sprinkles and Nhan Thanh Thi Nguyen Sprinkles to be identified as Author of this work has been asserted by him in accordance with the Copyright, Designs and Patents Act 1988.

A CIP catalogue record for this book is available from the British Library

All rights reserved. No part of this book may be reproduced or transmitted in any form or by any means, electronic or mechanical including photocopying, recording or by any information storage and retrieval system, without permission from the Publisher in writing.

Typeset in INDIA by IMPEC eSolutions
Printed and bound in the England by CPI Group (UK) Ltd, Croydon, CR0 4YY

Pen & Sword Books Ltd. incorporates the Imprints of Pen & Sword Archaeology, Atlas, Aviation, Battleground, Discovery, Family History, History, Maritime, Military, Naval, Politics, Railways, Select, Transport, True Crime, Fiction, Frontline Books, Leo Cooper, Praetorian Press, Seaforth Publishing, Wharncliffe, White Owl and After the Battle.

For a complete list of Pen & Sword titles please contact

PEN & SWORD BOOKS LIMITED
47 Church Street, Barnsley, South Yorkshire S70 2AS, United Kingdom
E-mail: enquiries@pen-and-sword.co.uk
Website: www.pen-and-sword.co.uk

Or

PEN AND SWORD BOOKS
1950 Lawrence Rd, Havertown, PA 19083, USA
E-mail: Uspen-and-sword@casematepublishers.com
Website: www.penandswordbooks.com

This book is dedicated to my beautiful wife's (Nhan Thanh Thi Nguyen) parents, her mother La Thi Nguyen and father Chi Huu Nguyen and her brother Cuong Huu Nguyen (R.I.P.), who was a hero for Vietnam as an engineer pilot that served in the Vietnam Air Force and died in a plane crash on 22 February 1984 over the Pacific Ocean while performing a mission. Chi Huu's parents had to live through the Japanese occupation of Vietnam during the Second World War. It is a miracle that they survived. I love my wife and her family for they are my family now as well.

Contents

Preface		ix
Chapter I	General William 'Billy' Mitchell's Pearl Harbor Predictions, 1925	1
Chapter II	The Tanaka Memorial, 1927	13
Chapter III	Pearl Harbor Naval War Games, 1932	81
Chapter IV	Japanese Naval Academy Pearl Harbor Question of 1935/Unit 731	89
Chapter V	The Attack on USS *Panay*, 1937	94
Chapter VI	The Nanking Massacre, 1937–38	100
Chapter VII	Pearl Harbor Naval War Games Fleet Exercise XIX of 1938	107
Chapter VIII	Warning to FDR by Admiral Richardson, October 1940	110
Chapter IX	Japan 1940 Onward/FDR's Secret Ways to Get Japan in the War	118
Chapter X	Breaking Japan's Codes	130
Chapter XI	Memos and Warnings to the Commanders at Pearl Harbor, 1941	136
Chapter XII	Attack on Pearl Harbor, 1941	152
Chapter XIII	FDR's Meeting with Edward Morrow and Colonel William Donovan, 1941	188

Chapter XIV 1941 to Present: The United States Cover-up   192
Chapter XV   Conclusion   198

Notes   214
Final Thoughts   219
Bibliography   220
About the Authors 225

Preface

To many students of history it would seem that the attack by the Japanese on Pearl Harbor in December of 1941 would be cut and dried. To them and other average scholars and historians it was nothing more than a surprise attack by the Japanese Navy on the American naval base at Pearl Harbor in the Hawaiian Islands. However, when a true historian examines all the evidence, a whole new picture begins to emerge and a student of history can see that this was no surprise attack in the broadest sense of the term.

The timeline to the events that led up to the attack on Pearl Harbor is truly amazing. What is so remarkable is that no one has ever tried to connect the dots to these events to show that either Franklin Delano Roosevelt was the least effective President that the United States ever had, or he knew and allowed the attack on Pearl Harbor to take place knowing it would cost thousands of American lives, not just at Pearl Harbor but at the United States Army base in the Philippines.

Americans and history students seem to forget that after the Japanese attacked Pearl Harbor they launched an attack on the Philippine Islands, which would lead to General Douglas MacArthur making a narrow escape. The remaining soldiers, sailors, and marines then had to survive more than four months of fighting before surrendering and enduring the 'Bataan Death March', which very few survived. Then they would have to try to live out the war as prisoners of war (PoWs) of the brutal Japanese.

The other thing that historians and scholars seem to forget is that FDR could have possibly got these men out in December right after the attack and saved many of their lives. Yet he did not even try and he would order MacArthur to escape, against his wishes. The point to be made here is that none of this had to happen because the United States could have been at war with Japan as early as 1937. This book will explore all of these facts from 1925 to the present.

Chapter I

General William 'Billy' Mitchell's Pearl Harbor Predictions, 1925

Brigadier General William 'Billy' Mitchell was a thorn in the side of his superiors due to the fact that he wanted to make a stronger Army and Navy Air Force. His arrogant behaviour towards his superiors did not help his position either. However, in his book *Wing Defense* he correctly predicted the attack by the Japanese on the Hawaiian Islands in December 1941.

In autumn 1923, Mitchell, then Assistant Chief of the young Army Air Service, was sent on an inspection tour of the Pacific. Upon his return, he publicly voiced opinions about the inadequacies of the United States' Pacific defences and the very real threat of Japanese aggression. His claims caused a furore in the War Department and would lead to him being court-martialled.

Among other things, Mitchell warned that the Hawaiian Islands – and, in particular, the great naval base at Pearl Harbor – were open to a Japanese surprise air attack. He then proceeded to outline how such an attack could be made successfully. Because Mitchell failed to reckon on the development of the aircraft carrier, many details of his plan now seem unnecessarily elaborate, if not fantastic; but in the light of what happened on 7 December 1941, his total concept proved alarmingly accurate.

Mitchell had set the date of the attack as early December 1941. This prediction came sixteen years before the attack was made on Pearl Harbor. Mitchell believed that a surprise attack on the Hawaiian Islands would be conducted by land-based aircraft operating from islands in the Pacific. His report, published in 1925 as the book *Winged*

Defense, foretold wider benefits of an investment in air power, believing it at the time, and for the future, 'a dominating factor in the world's development', both for national defence and economic benefit. *Winged Defense* sold only 4,500 copies between August 1925 and January 1926, the months surrounding the publicity of his court martial, and so Mitchell did not reach a wide audience.

In 1924 General Pershing, perhaps to keep Mitchell out of harm's way, sent him out on an inspection tour of the Pacific. In his notes of that tour, later reduced to a 323-page report, Mitchell took a look at the weakness of the US in the Pacific and the rising power of Japan. He predicted war between Japan and the US, and a Japanese strike on Pearl Harbor and Clark Field in the Philippines: Again it must be stated for clarity that this was sixteen years before Japan attacked Pearl Harbor:

Japan knows full well that the United States will probably enter the next war with the methods and weapons of the former war. It also knows full well that the defense of the Hawaiian group is based on the island of Oahu and not on the defense of the whole group.

The Japanese bombardment, (would be) 100 (air) ships organized into four squadrons of 25 (air) ships each. The objectives for attack are: Ford Island, airdrome, hangers, storehouses and ammunition dumps; Navy fuel oil tanks; also:

1. Water supply of Honolulu;
2. Water supply of Schofield;
3. Schofield Barracks airdrome and troop establishments;
4. Naval submarine station;
5. City and wharves of Honolulu.

Attack will be launched as follows: bombardment, attack to be made on Ford Island at 7:30 a.m. Attack to be made on Clark Field (Philippine Islands) at 10:40 a.m.

Japanese pursuit aviation will meet bombardment over Clark Field, proceeding in squadrons, one at 3000 feet to Clark Field from the southeast and with the sun at their back, one at 5000 feet from the north and one at 10,000 feet from the west. Should U.S. pursuit to destroy or fail to appear, airdrome would be attacked with machineguns. The (Japanese) air force would then carry out a systematic siege against Corregidor.

This is from *Winged Defense* and Mitchell's report. It is important and that is why the basic plan has been shown both from the initial report and the published one.

In his hypothetical attack times Mitchell was only twenty-five minutes off in regard to Pearl Harbor and two hours in regard to Clark Field. Ironically these predictions were used in his court martial by the prosecution in an attempt to show that Mitchell was an unstable publicity hound. Mitchell died in 1936 and thus did not live to see his unheeded predictions turn into grim prophecy.[1]

The other thing that needs to be remembered here is that Mitchell also listed the date of the attack on Pearl Harbor by the Japanese as early December 1941. He would later be promoted, (after his death) to major general and President Harry Truman would award him a Gold Medal for Bravery (the only one of its kind), which was presented to his family after the Second World War.

The question that should be asked here of FDR if this report was available from 1925, yet he did not consult it or even have his commanders review it, is why? This is a question that needs to be answered. As any scholar or historian will understand, this book is going to present a hypothesis as to why FDR either ignored this report or knew about it and refused to do anything about what it was testifying to regarding what the Japanese were planning or what the United States should do to avoid an attack. Also, why was the top brass so eager to court martial Mitchell when Douglas MacArthur, who was sitting in judgment, would vote for an acquittal? It is true that Mitchell was an arrogant officer, but then again almost every general to ever serve in the American military has been of this nature. One only has to look at MacArthur, Patton, Lee, Grant, Custer, Bradley, and Halsey just to name a few. The fact that the commanders who court-martialled Mitchell were never held accountable for their actions and that these actions would lead to the loss of thousands of men's lives at Pearl Harbor and in the Philippines is a great example of how politicians and military leaders cover up the facts of a historical event by not reporting it or even lying about it.

What enraged Mitchell as much as anything was the public reaction of Secretary of the Navy Curtis D. Wilbur, who said the accidents illustrated the limitations of air power. 'Some people,' said Wilbur, 'make extravagant claims for aviation. Great things have been achieved. From our experience, however, I am convinced that the Atlantic and the Pacific are still the greatest bulwarks against any air invasion of the United States.' Wilbur said the PN-9 incident, in which a flying boat on a flight from California to Hawaii was forced to land on the sea and the crew then spent nine days adrift, showed how difficult it was to cross 2,100 miles of ocean without carrying bombs, much less to cross with 1,000lb bombs.

On 5 September 1925 in San Antonio, Mitchell called in the press and gave them a 5,000-word statement. 'These accidents are the direct result of the incompetency, criminal negligence, and almost treasonable administration of the national defense by the Navy and War Departments,' he said.

'All aviation policies, schemes, and systems are dictated by non-flying officers of the Army or Navy who know practically nothing about it,' he said. 'The lives of the airmen are being used merely as pawns in their hands ... Officers and agents sent by the War and Navy Departments to Congress have almost always given incomplete, misleading, or false information about aeronautics.' Mitchell said *Shenandoah*, overweight in its structure and with low reserve buoyancy, had been sent on a propaganda mission without adequate safeguards. He then moved on to general criticism of Army and Navy aviation programmes.

He wasn't finished.

Four days later, he called the reporters back and said, 'If the department does not like the statement I made, let them take disciplinary action as they see fit, according to their judgment, court martial or no court martial ... The investigation that is needed is of the War and Navy Departments and their conduct in the disgraceful administration of aviation.' Summoned to Washington to explain himself, Mitchell was greeted at the train station by cheering supporters and an American Legion fife and drum corps.

Orders from Coolidge

President Calvin Coolidge was Mitchell's direct opposite in personality. A dour man of few words, he was satisfied to be known as 'Silent Cal'. He made his national reputation by putting down a police strike in Boston in 1919 when he was governor of Massachusetts. The War Department inspector general recommended that Mitchell be tried by court martial. The charges were not made by Mitchell's military superior but rather by the Secretary of War at the direction of the President. Coolidge did not accuse Mitchell directly in public. That might have been seen as prejudicing the outcome of the trial. However, there was no doubt who Coolidge was talking about when he spoke to the American Legion convention in early October. 'Any organisation of men in the military service bent on inflaming the public mind for the purpose of forcing government action through the pressure of public opinion is an exceedingly dangerous undertaking and precedent,' Coolidge said. 'It is for the civil authority to determine what appropriations shall be granted, what appointments shall be made, and what rules shall be adopted for the conduct of its armed forces ... Whenever the military power starts dictating to the civil authority by whatever means adopted, the liberties of the country are beginning to end.'

Mitchell was charged under the 96th Article of War, the catch-all general article that covered 'disorders and neglects to the prejudice of good order and discipline [and] all conduct of a nature to bring discredit upon the military service.' Mitchell ridiculed Article 96, saying, 'Officers are tried under it for kicking a horse.' The Army held Mitchell's statements were prejudicial to good order and discipline, insubordinate, 'contemptuous and disrespectful', and intended to discredit the War Department and Navy Department. With the 5 and 9 September statements counted separately, it added up to eight specifications to the charge.

Coolidge, hoping to tamp down the controversy and divert attention from the Mitchell court martial, appointed a board, headed by New York banker Dwight W. Morrow, to look into the military aviation issue.

Curtain Up

The court martial began on 28 October in the Emery Building, an old red brick warehouse at the foot of Capitol Hill in downtown Washington. Five hundred people, including forty reporters and newsreel cameramen, lined the streets to see Colonel Mitchell and his wife arrive. Twelve senior generals, handpicked by the Army and the War Department, were appointed to the court. One of them, destined for greater things, was Mitchell's boyhood friend from Milwaukee, Douglas MacArthur. In addition, there was a 'law member' of the court, Colonel Blanton C. Winship, a legal officer assigned to assist and rule on legal questions. Mitchell promptly challenged three of the generals off the court, including Major General Charles P. Summerall, a future Army Chief of Staff who was to have been president of the court. The ousted generals were not replaced, as only six members were required for a trial. Major General Robert L. Howze took over as president.

Mitchell's defence team was led by Representative Frank R. Reid (Republican, Illinois.), a first-rate lawyer who had met Mitchell at House Aircraft Committee hearings. He called members of the court 'you men' and 'you people', but the generals took it in their stride. The prosecutor was the trial judge advocate Colonel Sherman Moreland, fully competent but no match for Reid in flash and dash. Photos from the trial show members of the court with old-style high military collars. Mitchell wore his collar folded down in the more modern fashion favoured by airmen, who claimed that high collars chafed their necks while flying. The prosecution introduced its evidence on the morning of 2 November and rested its case that afternoon. Moreland called witnesses who established that Mitchell made the two statements and gave them to the press. In the Army's view, this was prima facie breach of good order and discipline and sufficient for conviction. It was not nearly over, though.

The next day, Reid announced that he wanted to call seventy-three witnesses for the defence and asked for thousands of Army documents. He intended to argue the validity of what Mitchell had said. Moreland objected. All that mattered was Mitchell had made the statements. The substance of what he said counted only for mitigation and extenuation, if that.

However, the court did not rule against the evidence Reid wanted to present. Under the glare of public and press attention, Mitchell was given leeway that he would not have got under other circumstances. Reid and Mitchell had effectively converted the court martial into a public debate about air power. The trial would continue for six more weeks.

Gullion Evens the Odds

Reid introduced a parade of witnesses who gave evidence about equipment, training, misleading military assessments to Congress, Army disregard of advice from air officers, and endangerment of pilots from orders by non-flying superiors. He established that in the past seven years, Mitchell had made 163 recommendations to improve the air service, nearly all of them ignored or disapproved. A surprise witness was Margaret Lansdowne, widow of the commander of the USS *Shenandoah*, an airship that had crashed in a storm in Ohio in 1925. She testified the Navy tried to influence her statement to the board of inquiry, wanting her to say that her husband had been willing and ready to make the flight. She told the inquiry and the Mitchell court that her husband had regarded the flight as political and had flown it under protest, believing the timing was dangerous because of the weather risk. She produced a copy of a letter from Lieutenant Commander Zachary Lansdowne to the Chief of Naval Operations asking for a delay until thunderstorm season had passed.

Among those testifying for Mitchell were First World War ace Eddie Rickenbacker and Congressman Fiorello La Guardia. 'Billy Mitchell is not being judged by his peers,' La Guardia said. 'He is being judged by nine dog robbers of the general staff.' Two little-known majors, Henry H. 'Hap' Arnold and Carl A. Spaatz, appeared for Mitchell as well. Even the court was momentarily star struck when famed humourist Will Rogers, a friend of Mitchell's, attended a session of the trial.

Mitchell was the runaway favourite of the public, but the weeks of air power testimony made less of an impression on the members of the court, who understood better than the civilians did the meaning of an Article 96 charge. To shore up the prosecution, Major Allen W. Gullion was added as an assistant trial judge advocate on 17 November. A West Pointer and a former infantry officer, Gullion was regarded as one of the best and most aggressive prosecutors in the Army. The attack on Mitchell and the defence witnesses sharpened as Gullion took on a big share of the questioning. The trial reached its dramatic peak in late November when Gullion cross-examined Mitchell. He elicited acknowledgments from Mitchell that a considerable part of his statements were opinion rather than fact and that he relied on the newspapers for some of his information, especially about the Navy. Gullion tried to force Mitchell to admit that he had accused officers of long and honourable standing of treason and criminal actions. Mitchell said his words had been directed at a system rather than against an individual or individuals, but Gullion had scored his point with the senior officers on the court. The prosecution called a succession of rebuttal witnesses. Mitchell debunkers were not difficult to find. As the trial ground on, the Morrow Board made its report, basically accepting the arguments of the traditionalists over those of the airmen. No radical changes were necessary. The nation was safe from air attack. The Army and Navy air arms should stay where they were.

Summing up for the prosecution on the last day of the court martial, Gullion pulled out all the stops: 'It is sufficient if the record shows that the conduct is to the prejudice and of a nature to discredit,' he said.

'The statements of September 5 and 9 speak for themselves in that regard. But can there be any doubt that the discipline of our Army will be ruined if the accused, in the expressive vernacular of the doughboy, is allowed to get away with it? Every trooper in Fort Huachuca, as he smokes his cigarette after mess, is talking about this case. If the accused is not dismissed, the good trooper will be dismayed and the malcontent and sorehead will be encouraged in his own insubordination.'

Mitchell Leaves the Army

After deliberating for three hours on the afternoon of 17 December, the court found Mitchell guilty on the charge and all specifications. It suspended him from rank, command, and duty, with the forfeiture of all pay and allowances for five years. The votes were never revealed but Howze, the president of the court, said it was a split decision. It was widely believed that MacArthur had voted to acquit, but according to most historical sources that was never confirmed. In his memoirs, MacArthur was cryptic on the subject, saying, 'I did what I could in his behalf.' In November 1945, Senator Alexander Wiley (Republican, Wisconsin) – who was trying to get Mitchell promoted posthumously to major general – wrote to MacArthur, saying, 'It was my understanding that yours was the one vote against the court martial's verdict which cashiered Billy Mitchell.' MacArthur replied, 'Your recollection of my part in his trial is entirely correct. It was fully known to him, and he never ceased to express his gratitude for my attitude … He was a rare genius in his profession and contributed much to aviation history.'

Coolidge approved the conviction on 25 January 1926, saying that Mitchell 'employed expressions which cannot be construed otherwise than as breathing defiance toward his military superiors'.

However, Coolidge recognised that the sentence left Mitchell in an impossible situation. It kept him in service, which prevented him from obtaining private employment, but took away his pay, so he had no means of support. Coolidge reduced the punishment to forfeiture of half of Mitchell's monthly pay. The free-spending Mitchell could not get by on half pay and the net effect was to force him to resign from the Army, which he did on 1 February.

Pershing, now retired, observed, 'There seems to be a Bolshevik bug in the air.' With Mitchell gone, the Army cracked down on dissent. Arnold, an activist on Mitchell's behalf, was exiled to Fort Riley, Kansas, a cavalry post, where he became commander of an observation squadron. Some airmen concurred in Mitchell's conviction. Benjamin D. Foulois, who had despised Mitchell since their time in France in the First World War, said, 'A civilian could say things like that but not an officer on active duty that had obligated himself by his commissioning oath to an unswerving course of loyalty to his civilian and military superiors.' In his memoirs, Arnold acknowledged as much. 'No matter what was said about "Airpower being on trial" – as it was, at times even in the eyes of the prosecution – the thing for which Mitchell was really being tried he was guilty of, and except for Billy, everybody knew it,' Arnold said. 'We all knew there was no other way – in accordance with the Army code, Billy had it coming.'

Reconsiderations

Mitchell continued to speak, write, and advocate for air power. He died in 1936, but as his disciples, including Arnold and Spaatz, moved into positions of authority, he was openly acknowledged as an Air Force hero. When the Air Force Association was formed in 1946, Mitchell became AFA's hero, too. And when the Air Force gained its independence from the Army in 1947, the cover of the association's journal, *Air Force Magazine*, proclaimed it 'The Day Billy Mitchell Dreamed Of'. In 1956, William Mitchell Jr, with AFA acting as his agent, petitioned the Air Force Board for Correction of Military Records to overturn the verdict of the court martial. The board heard the case in 1957, but the results were not disclosed until the final review in 1958. By a vote of four-to-one, the board recommended the findings and sentence of the court martial be declared null and void. 'The conclusion is inescapable in the board's opinion that Mitchell was tried for his views rather than a violation of Article 96,' the proceedings report said.

Secretary of the Air Force James H. Douglas Jr could not agree. He recognised that many of Mitchell's beliefs had been vindicated by history but that 'while on active duty and subject to the discipline of military service, he characterized the administration of the War and Navy Departments as incompetent, criminally negligent, and almost treasonable'. Mitchell's statements in September 1925 substantiated the charges against him. 'Subsequent confirmation of the correctness of certain views he expressed cannot affect the propriety or impropriety under the 96th Article of expressions which he employed.' The verdict stood. The Mitchell issue was supposedly settled, but popped up again in a different form in 2004. The Fiscal 2005 Defense Authorization bill authorised the promotion of Billy Mitchell to major general, effective as of the date of his death in 1936. However, neither the Pentagon nor the White House took any action as a result of the authorisation and the matter is again at rest – at least, so far.'[2]

As anyone can see, Mitchell was used as a scapegoat for the Army and Navy not wanting to make a stronger Army and Navy Air Force. The question remains, why FDR when he became President did not do anything to make the United States Navy and Army Air Force stronger and more capable than it was? The answer from my perspective as a historian and scholar is that FDR was setting Pearl Harbor up for an attack from Japan. As a scholar it is important here to restate what General Mitchell was trying to get out in his report. The report's most important objective was to try and wise up the admirals and generals of the United States Navy and Army to build a stronger Air Force to defend against any attack that could come from any enemy of the United States. Mitchell did not want the United States to be caught with its pants down so to speak.

The information was right there in plain view for FDR to see and yet as President he did nothing to increase the defence from the air for the United States. He would allow the soldiers and sailors at Pearl Harbor to become sitting ducks to an attack from the Imperial Japanese Navy. This will be pointed out quite correctly in the chapters to come. Politically correct historians have tried to paint Franklin D. Roosevelt as a hero and the greatest President the United States ever had. This is far from the truth, as the evidence will show. In the aftermath of Pearl Harbor and the invasion of the Philippines, the Americans at these posts did not have to lose their lives and any scholar only has to study the facts to see a different outcome could have been possible.

Chapter II

The Tanaka Memorial, 1927

Any historian who has ever truly studied Japan's history should come to the escapable conclusion that this document is real. Scholars such as Hampton Sides, PhD Lester Tenney, Hal Gold and others profess that this document is real. Even today Japan honours its mass murderers from the Second World War at the Yasukuni Shrine. Today it amazes me that we still hunt down Nazi war criminals in their late 90s but allow Japanese war criminals to go free. Below is part of an essay written in 1940 by Russian revolutionary and scholar Leon Trotsky on the Tanaka Memorial. Also included in the article is the full Tanaka Memorial manuscript and it is a must read:

> The famous *Tanaka Memorial* was a document submitted to the Japanese emperor in 1927 by Baron Tanaka, the premier of Japan. This document outlined in detailed steps a program of Japanese imperialist expansion, beginning with establishment of Japanese control in Manchuria and leading eventually to domination of all China, Indonesia, the South Sea Islands, the Maritime Provinces of USSR and, eventually, India and the whole Pacific basin.
>
> Baron Tanaka even visualized ultimate Japanese control of Europe.
>
> When the document came to light, its authenticity was denied in Japan. But beginning in 1931 with the invasion of Manchuria, Japan proceeded along precisely the lines laid down in the *Tanaka Memorial*.

Yet the chancelleries of all the great imperialist powers and the Kremlin too, although certain of the authenticity of the 'Tanaka Memorial,' have remained silent while Japan has continued to deny its authenticity. Washington and London, engaged in 'appeasing' Japan – i.e., preparing for the most propitious moment for war in the Pacific – have discouraged publication of material on the *Tanaka Memorial*. The Soviet press likewise remains silent.

In the following article Leon Trotsky has told for the first time the story of how the *Tanaka Memorial* was secured by the Soviet intelligence service from the archives of the Japanese government. Comrade Trotsky had not quite finished this article when he was assassinated by Stalin's GPU.

The article was written for publication for the general public. Comrade Trotsky was still attempting to establish more specific dates for certain of the events. Although his memory was excellent, he was never satisfied, in anything he wrote, until he secured documentary verification. The editors have not been able to supplement Trotsky's own tentative dates with further verification.

In an article published in *Liberty on* 27 January 1940, Comrade Trotsky predicted that a forthcoming Kremlin-Japan pact 'would constitute a symmetric supplement to the pact between Moscow and Berlin.' Such a pact was actually signed on April 13, 1941. The Kremlin would scarcely vouch for the authenticity of the *Tanaka Memorial* today, for then it would be hard put to justify to the world working class the signing of the pact with Japan in the midst of China's struggle against Japanese imperialism. – *The Editors*

The American press has up to now considered the *Tanaka Memorial* a dubious document. On April 23, 1940, Rear Admiral Taussig referred to the *Tanaka Memorial* in his extremely interesting report to the Senate Committee on Naval Affairs. Rear Admiral Taussig was disavowed by his own department. It is not my intention to enter into this controversy. I believe that Rear Admiral Taussig had his own reasons for speaking, and the Navy Department had its own reasons for disavowing his views. Quite possibly the disavowal did not come as a surprise to the Rear Admiral. But, I repeat, this does not concern me. So far as I am able to judge, Rear Admiral Taussig is a qualified expert on the morals, tasks and politics of the Far East. He does not doubt the authenticity of the *Tanaka Memorial*. The *New York Times*, however, in reporting this session of the Senate Committee on Naval Affairs, found it necessary to remind its readers once again that the 'Japanese have always insisted that the so-called *Tanaka Memorial* was a Chinese forgery.' Thus even today, some sixteen years after the publication of the *Tanaka Memorial*, it still remains a suspect and controversial document.

The *Tanaka Memorial* is not a forgery. A careful analysis of its contents and text in and of itself testifies adequately to this. Moreover, the author of these lines is in possession of facts which verify completely and incontrovertibly the authenticity of the *Tanaka Memorial*.

Its Internal Validity
A genius in the fabrication of forgeries would have been required to execute so complex a forgery with such penetration into the objective situation and the political psychology of Japan's ruling circles. However, geniuses do not as a rule occupy themselves with forgeries but devote their energies to other pursuits. To be sure, there was no scarcity of forgeries during the last war and the ensuing post-war years. Suffice it to recall the notorious Sisson documents on the Soviet Republic. As a general rule – and I know of no exceptions – documents of this type are extremely crude. They tend to reveal the psychology of the

forgers themselves or of the circles for which they are intended rather than the psychology of those individuals or groups in whose name the forgeries are committed. If such documents meet with credibility, it is only because of lack of familiarity with the milieu from which they reportedly emanate. The Soviet Government consisted of individuals completely unknown to world public opinion. It's a small wonder that it was possible to ascribe to them any goal or aim whatsoever, and depict these things in any kind of language.

It is otherwise with the Imperial Government of Japan. It constitutes an ancient and traditional milieu. Whoever has carefully followed the evolution of Japanese politics cannot fail to acknowledge that the document, with its cynical realism and icy fanaticism of the ruling caste, originates in this milieu. The document is credible. The text is valid. The contents gain credence because they speak for themselves.

Japan is today the weakest link in the imperialist chain. Her financial and military superstructure rests on a foundation of semi-feudal agrarian barbarism. Periodical explosions within the Japanese army are only a reflection of the intolerable tension of social contradictions in the country. The regime as a whole maintains itself only through the dynamics of military seizures. The programmatic basis for these seizures is supplied by the *Tanaka Memorial*.

As I recall it, the 'Memorial' is based on the testament of Emperor Meiji. This testament itself is of course a myth. But Japanese aggression is interlaced with traditionalism. While creating a gigantic fleet of the most modern type, the Japanese imperialists prefer to base their activities on ancient national traditions. Just as priests put their pronouncements and desires into the mouths of deities, so do the Japanese imperialists palm off their very modern plans and combinations as the will of the august progenitors of the reigning Emperor. Similarly Tanaka covered up the imperialist aspirations of the ruling cliques by reference to a non-existing testament of an Emperor.

The document did not leap full-blown from Baron Tanaka's brow. It constitutes a generalization of the plans formulated by the Army and Navy leaders and, in a certain sense, reconciliation and a theoretical summation of these plans. It is to be assumed that many variants preceded the final draft; and that many discussions were held in intimate, 'non-official' and hence all the more influential circles. The task was to affix the seal of imperial will upon these aspirations of the Army and Navy circles. The old Emperor's physical and mental condition was such that his signature could not prove authoritative for the initiated. That is why the imperialist conspirators waited for the enthronement of Emperor Hirohito before presenting for his signature the document, which from all indications had received its final formulation under General Tanaka's direction.

Why I Can Verify its Authenticity
However, apart from these general considerations, the writer of these lines is able to vouch for the following facts. The *Tanaka Memorial* was first photographed in Tokyo in the Ministry of Naval Affairs and brought to Moscow as an undeveloped film. I was perhaps the very first person to become acquainted with the document in English and Russian translations of the Japanese text.

At that time relations with Japan were extremely alarming for Soviet foreign policy. The Far East was defended poorly. The defenses of the Chinese Eastern Railway were even worse. There was no talk in those days of selling the railway to the Japanese. Not so much because Moscow was not ready to sell, but primarily because Tokyo had no inclination to buy: they were preparing to get it free of charge.

Throughout that period Moscow made persistent offers to conclude a mutual non-aggression pact with Tokyo. These proposals were diplomatically evaded by Tokyo on the pretext that the time was not yet ripe for such a treaty. In those days treaties were still approached with a semblance of seriousness. In a few years it was already to become the rule that a mutual non-aggression pact was the best prelude to military invasion. In those years, however, Japan at all events preferred to evade.

Moscow never removed its eyes from the East. On the one hand there was the constant threat of Japanese plans. On the other hand, the Chinese Revolution of 1925–1927 was germinating. Great hopes were bound up with the Chinese Revolution, including the security of the Soviet Far Eastern possessions and the Chinese Eastern Railway. The writer was not among those on the government staff who believed that the Chinese Eastern Railway must be handed over to the Japanese as soon as the latter succeeded in gaining control of Manchuria.

But neither the duration of the Chinese Revolution nor its success was guaranteed in advance. Japanese militarism was an existing fact, very palpable, very aggressive. The Chinese Revolution was a question of the future. It is hardly astonishing that the Soviet Intelligence Service in both its branches – that which fulfilled military assignments and that of the GPU – were under orders to watch carefully every Japanese move in diplomatic as well as military fields.

The Military Intelligence Service was under a two-fold jurisdiction: subject on the one hand to the War Department and on the other to the GPU. The Foreign Department of the GPU was headed by an old Bolshevik, Trilisser, who was later removed and apparently liquidated along with many others. The Military Intelligence was headed by Berzin, an old Lettish Bolshevik. I was not closely acquainted with the organization of our agency in Japan, being little interested in the technical aspects of the matter. I handed this over to my aides, first Sklyansky, later Unschlicht and, to a certain extent, Rosenholtz. Permit me to recall that Sklyansky, one of the outstanding and most meritorious organizers of the Red Army, was drowned in 1924 or 1925 in America while taking a boat ride on a lake. Unschlicht disappeared, and was evidently liquidated. Rosenholtz was shot by verdict of the court.

Questions relating to the Intelligence Service were thus brought to my attention only in exceptional cases involving issues of great military or political importance. This is precisely what happened on the occasion to which I have referred.

Early Soviet Advantages in Intelligence Work
The successes of which the Soviet Foreign Intelligence could already boast at that time were by no means accidental. The party had at its disposal not a few people who had passed through a serious conspiratorial school and who were well acquainted with all the methods and subterfuges of the police and counter-espionage. They brought into their work an international experience, many of them having been émigrés in various lands and possessing a broad political outlook. They had personal friends in many countries. Nor was there any lack of self-sacrificing support on the part of the revolutionary elements in different countries. In many government institutions of capitalist countries the lower functionaries were sympathetic to a considerable degree to the October revolution. Provided one knew how, their sympathy could be utilized in the interests of the Soviet power. It was so utilized.

The network of foreign agencies was still very little developed, far from complete but, by way of compensation, lucky individual connections sometimes produced unexpected and extraordinary results.

Dzerzhinsky, the then head of the GPU, used to refer with satisfaction on more than one occasion to the extraordinary sources of information at his disposal in Japan.

Despite the shut-in character of the Japanese, and their ability to keep secrets – which arises from the specific, special conditions of their national milieu and the inaccessibility of the Japanese language to the overwhelming majority of foreigners – it must be said that this ability is nevertheless not absolute. The decomposition of the old system finds its expression not only in the fact that young officers and officials from time to time shoot Ministers whom they find inconvenient but also in this that other less patriotic officers and officials wearied of Spartan customs seek for sources of revenue on the side. I know of cases of important Japanese functionaries, assigned to work in Japanese Consulates in European countries, who gave up important secrets for relatively modest sums of money.

Dzerzhinsky was brought into the Political Bureau after Lenin's death. This step was taken by Stalin, Zinoviev and Kamenev in order to attract to their side the honest but vainglorious Dzerzhinsky. They succeeded completely.

Dzerzhinsky was very talkative, very hot-tempered and explosive. This man of iron will who had served terms of hard penal labor possessed traits which were absolutely childlike. Once during a session of the Political Bureau he boasted of his hopes shortly to lure Boris Savinkov to Soviet soil and arrest him. My reaction to this was highly skeptical. But Dzerzhinsky proved right. Savinkov was lured by agents of the GPU to Soviet territory and arrested there. Shortly thereafter Dzerzhinsky expressed his hopes of apprehending Wrangel in the same way. But this hope did not materialize because Wrangel proved more cautious.

Very often, without giving any technical details, into which no one even inquired, he would boast of the successes of our foreign espionage, especially in Japan.

One day in 1925, in the summer or early autumn, Dzerzhinsky talked excitedly about his expectations of obtaining an extremely important document from Japan. He stated ecstatically that this document in and of itself could provoke international upheavals, events of vast importance, war between Japan and the United States, etc. I remained, as always in such cases, even more skeptical.

'Wars are not provoked by documents,' I objected to Dzerzhinsky. But he insisted: 'You have no conception of the importance of this document; it is the program of the ruling circles, approved by the Mikado himself; it embraces the seizure of China, the destruction of the United States, world domination.'

'Mightn't your agent be duped?' I asked. 'No one writes such documents as a rule. Why should such plans be put down on paper?'

Dzerzhinsky was himself not very sure on this point. He replied, as if to dispel the doubts in his own mind: 'In their country they do everything in the name of the Emperor. In order to justify risky measures, risky politics and vast army and naval expenditures the military men and the diplomats have been seeking to tempt the Mikado with a colossal perspective which is equally indispensable to themselves for the political adventures in which they are engaging. That is why Tanaka has written down the plans of the military circles in a special report to the Emperor, and this report has met with the Emperor's approval. We will receive a photographic copy of the document directly from the archives of the Ministry of Foreign Affairs.'

How the Document Was Secured
I remember that Dzerzhinsky mentioned a sum to be paid for the photographic copy. It was relatively modest, about three thousand American dollars.

From Dzerzhinsky I learned that the GPU enjoyed the services of a very trusted functionary who had direct access to the secret archives of the Japanese Ministry of Foreign Affairs. In a period of more than a year he had already provided some very valuable information and was marked by great precision and conscientiousness in fulfilling his obligations as a foreign spy. He was quite familiar with the archives and with the relative importance of the various documents. This functionary had proposed to copy the document but the GPU representative, upon instructions from Moscow, demanded photographic copies. This was much more difficult. It was necessary to introduce a GPU technician into the premises of the Ministry or to teach the functionary the art of photography. These technical difficulties caused a delay in obtaining the document. Several copies of each page were taken, and the film was then forwarded by two or three different routes. All the copies arrived safely in Moscow.

I must admit that I am unable now to recall, perhaps I was not interested in this at the time – whether the Japanese agent was one among the volunteers sincerely devoted to the new Soviet regime, or one of a number of hired agents or, finally, a type representing a combination of the two. This last type was probably the most prevalent. The number of sympathizers in Japan was very small.

'The document has arrived!' Dzerzhinsky announced joyously. Where was it? It had arrived as a film which was being developed. The developing was coming out successfully and the document was being translated by our Japanese experts as it was developed. They were all staggered by the contents of the very first few pages. I would get my report from Trilisser. (It might have been Unschlicht.)

As the head of the War Department, I was naturally interested in Far Eastern questions, but there was still another connection. During the first period of the Soviet regime, in the initial months up to February 1918, I was in charge of the Commissariat of Foreign Affairs. Upon arriving from England, Chicherin, whom we had exchanged for several arrested Englishmen, became my deputy. When I shifted to the War Department, Chicherin, who had been coping successfully with his assignment, was appointed as the People's Commissar of Foreign Affairs on my motion in the Council of People's Commissars and in the Central Executive Committee of the Soviets. As a member of the Political Bureau I frequently used to draft together with Chicherin the more important diplomatic documents. On the other hand, in all cases where I required the aid of diplomacy during the civil war, I would get in touch directly with Chicherin.

In 1923 the 'Troika' (Zinoviev-Kamenev-Stalin) made an attempt to remove me from all supervision of foreign policy. This function was formally assigned to Zinoviev. Nevertheless the old relationships and, so to speak, the old unofficial hierarchy continued to remain in force. Even in 1925, after I had already left the War Department and was placed in charge of the modest Concessions Committee, I was, as a member of the Political Bureau, appointed head of the Committee on Far Eastern Affairs, Japan and China. Among the members of this Committee were Chicherin, Voroshilov, Krassin, Rudzutak and others.

Stalin was at that time still wary of venturing on the slippery ice of international politics. For the most part, he would listen and look on, formulate his opinion, or merely vote after others had expressed themselves.

Zinoviev, who was formally in charge of diplomatic affairs, was inclined, as everybody knew, to fall into a panic whenever a difficult situation arose. All this explains amply why the document received from Tokyo was transmitted directly to me.

We Study the Document

I must acknowledge that the vast scope of the plan, the cold and ruthless messianism of the Mikado's bureaucratic clique, astounded me. But the text of the document did not arouse in my mind the slightest doubt, not only because I was acquainted with the document's history but also because of its internal validity.

If we grant that the Chinese did manage to find an ideal forger who fabricated this document, then the question still remains just how did this Chinese forgery turn up in the Japanese Ministry of Foreign Affairs as a special, secret document? Did the Ministry of Foreign Affairs itself arrange to transmit the falsified Chinese document and pass it off as a genuine Japanese document? This supposition is utterly fantastic. The Japanese could not have been in the least interested in circulating such a document and arousing belief in it. They demonstrated this most graphically by branding it as a forgery the moment it was published.

The film was developed and the translation made at once in the offices of the Intelligence Service, and both were rushed immediately to the Kremlin. They were still wet and the translation was in the shape of the first rough draft. Many corrections were later required.

Did the other members of the Political Bureau become acquainted with the document at the same time as I did, or was it shortly after? I have no definite recollection on this point. In any case, when the Political Bureau met, all the members were acquainted with the document. Although personal relations were already very strained at that time, all the members of the Political Bureau seemed temporarily to draw closer together because of the document. In the preliminary discussion the main topic was naturally the veracity of the Japanese. The megalomania in which mysticism and cynicism remarkably supplemented each other was spoken of with astonishment tinged with grudging admiration.

'Isn't this perhaps a poem, a forgery?' asked Bukharin who with all his childlike gullibility loved, whenever a propitious occasion offered itself, to play the part of a cautious statesman. Dzerzhinsky exploded, as usual.

'I have already explained to you,' he said, speaking with a Polish accent which always became thicker as he grew excited, 'that this document is supplied by our agent who has proved his complete trustworthiness; and that this document was kept in the most secret section of the archives of the Naval Ministry. Our agent introduced our photographer into the premises. He himself didn't know how to operate a camera. Is it perhaps your opinion that the Japanese Admirals themselves placed a forged document in their secret archives? The Naval Ministry originally had no copy of this document. It was at first kept only in the Emperor's personal archives, with a copy in the Ministry of Foreign Affairs. Then the Army and Navy Ministries asked for their own copies. Our agent learned the exact time when a copy would arrive from the Ministry of Foreign Affairs. Extreme precautions were taken with its delivery. Our agent was able to gain access to it only thanks to the fact that a copy finally got into the archives of the Naval Ministry. Are you perhaps of the opinion that all this was done specially for purposes of fraud?'

As for myself, I had, I repeat, no doubts about its authenticity, if only on the basis of its internal validity. 'If we granted for a moment,' I said, 'that this document is a forgery then we must also grant that the forgery is the work of the Japanese themselves. What for? To sell it to us for two or three thousand dollars? Enrich the treasury of the Naval Ministry by three thousand dollars? Or do they desire in this way to provoke us, frighten us? But we are already aware of their appetites, although, to be sure, not on such a scale. They know that despite a whole series of provocations we are doing everything in our power to avoid a conflict. A programmatic document could not in any way cause a change in our policy.'

Discussion on this point ended quickly. All the circumstances and all the technical details, which have not of course been retained in my memory, left no room for doubts about the authenticity of the document.

What to do with the *Memorial*?
The question next arose: What to do? We had in our possession a charge of great explosive power. There was naturally danger that we might blow ourselves up. From every standpoint it was not expedient to publish it in the Soviet press. In the first place, this would reveal to the Japanese authorities that an agent of extraordinary value was at the disposal of our espionage. Dzerzhinsky would not agree to this in any case. Far more important were considerations of a political nature. Japan's plans were calculated for a number of decades. The Kremlin was concerned with gaining a few years, even a few months. We were sparing the Japanese in every way. We made very great concessions. Our wisest, most careful and mildest diplomat, Joffe, was functioning in Japan. The publication of this document in Moscow would be tantamount to saying openly to the Japanese that we were seeking a conflict. The scales would immediately tip in favor of the most bellicose circles in the Japanese army and navy. It was absolutely irrational to provoke Japan by publishing this document which, moreover, might not gain credence abroad.

Zinoviev at first made the proposal that the document be published in the periodical, *Communist International*. This method of publication would still leave the government itself on the side-lines. But no one would hear of it, nor did Zinoviev insist on his hasty proposal.

I offered a plan which I had elaborated before coming to the session of the Political Bureau. It was necessary to publish the document abroad, and avoid any link whatever between the document and Moscow, without lessening its effect, without arousing mistrust, without compromising the GPU agents in Japan. But where? The place of publication literally offered itself, namely, the United States. I proposed that, after the document was translated into English, it should be transmitted to the press by a trustworthy and authoritative friend of the Soviet Republic in the United States. At that time the calling of a friend of the Soviet Union had not yet become a profession. The number of friends was not large; important and influential personalities were all too scarce. In any case the task turned out much more difficult than I had presumed.

We were under the impression that the document would literally be torn from our hands. Dzerzhinsky had hopes of easily recouping the expenses of our Japanese agency. But things did not turn out that way at all. It was not easy to provide a credible version of how the document was obtained from Tokyo. Any reference to the real source, i.e., the GPU, would arouse additional mistrust. In America the suspicion would naturally arise that the GPU itself had simply manufactured the document in order to poison relations between Japan and the United States.

The English translation was painstakingly made in Moscow. That, together with the English text, were forwarded to New York, and in this way any trace of a connection between this document and Moscow were eliminated.

It should not be forgotten that this took place during the administration of President Coolidge and Secretary Hughes, that is, an administration very hostile to the Soviet Union. There was every justification to fear that hostile experts would simply pronounce the document a Moscow fabrication. It is a fact that fraudulent documents are sometimes acknowledged to be genuine while authentic documents are not infrequently as forgeries.

To my knowledge the American press made no references to Moscow as the key point from which the document was forwarded from Tokyo to New York. However, there was no 'malice' on the part of Moscow in this affair, unless of course it is considered as malicious to obtain a document from the secret archives of a hostile power. We were simply unable to devise any other way of bringing the document to the attention of world public opinion except by publishing it in the American press, without indicating the source, or rather by camouflaging the actual source as much as possible.

In those years the Soviet republic did not as yet have its own diplomatic representative in the United States; at the head of the Amtorg was the engineer, Bogdanov. He and his colleagues, who are today better known and more influential, fulfilled all sorts of diplomatic missions. I cannot now recall just who among them was entrusted with the task of finding a competent person among the Americans and putting the document in circulation through him. In any case it should not be difficult to verify this, since the document was offered to the most influential publications in the order of their importance.

According to certain indications the *Tanaka Memorial* was signed by the Mikado in July 1927. In that case it is quite obvious that the document was forwarded to Moscow prior to its being actually signed by the Mikado. The document, as has already been stated, had been under discussion among the close summits of the Japanese Army, the Navy and the diplomatic corps. It was precisely during this period that copies had to be made available to the Ministries concerned. Tanaka became premier in April 1927. He might have well obtained the post of Premier precisely because of undertaking to win the Emperor's sanction for this program of the extreme wing of the militarists and imperialists.

Why do the Japanese authorities pronounce the *Tanaka Memorial* a *Chinese* forgery? They were obviously unaware of Moscow's role in the publication of this document. The appearance of the *Memorial* in the American and not the Soviet press naturally inspired the idea that the *Memorial* had in some way fallen into Chinese hands who hastened to forward it to the United States.

Why is the Kremlin Silent?
It is hard to understand why Moscow, which is best informed on this matter, persists in maintaining silence about the *Tanaka Memorial*. The original photographic copy was received in Moscow under circumstances precluding any doubts whatever about its authenticity. This remarkable document was sent abroad, i.e., to the United States from Moscow, from the Kremlin. The authenticity of the document is strangely enough suspect even today. Moscow keeps quiet.

To be sure Moscow had ample reasons in its day to hide its participation in publishing and exposing the *Tanaka Memorial*. The prime consideration was not to provoke Tokyo. This explains why the Kremlin took the round-about way in making it public. But the situation has drastically changed in the decade and a half that has since elapsed. Moscow is very well aware that the technical conditions, the conspiratorial considerations which originally impelled the hiding of the source of information have long since disappeared: The individuals involved have been replaced (mostly shot), the methods have changed. The flight to Japan of General Luchkov, an important GPU functionary, marks a dividing line between two periods of espionage direction. Even if Luchkov did not surrender his former agents into the hands of the Japanese – and his conduct leads me to believe that he revealed everything he knew – Moscow must have hastily eliminated all agents and changed connections long ago, in view of the danger from Luchkov. From every aspect, the silence of the Kremlin is well-nigh incomprehensible.

One has to assume that operating here is the excessive caution which often drives Stalin to ignore major considerations for the sake of secondary and petty ones.

It is more than likely that this time too Moscow does not wish to cause any annoyances to Tokyo in view of the negotiations now under way in the hope of reaching a more stable and lasting agreement. All these considerations, however, recede to the background as the world war spreads its concentric circles ever wider and as Japan waits only an opportune moment in the Far East before taking the next step toward the realization of the *Tanaka Memorial*.

I ask myself: Why didn't I relate this episode before, an episode which throws light on one of the most important political documents of modern history? It was simply because no occasion arose for it. In the interval between the meeting of the Political Bureau in 1925 when the question of the Tanaka document first came up, and the period when I found myself in exile abroad and had the opportunity of following international affairs more accurately – in this interval there intervened the years of the cruel internal struggle, arrest, exile to Central Asia, and then Turkey. The Tanaka document remained dormant in the recesses of my memory.

The course of events in the Far East in recent years has corroborated the Tanaka program to such a degree as to preclude any doubts about the authenticity of this document.[1]

What Trotsky said is correct, this is not a forgery but a true document. Below you can read the Tanaka Memorial from the first page to the last and see for yourself exactly what Japan had planned as early as

The Tanaka Memorial, 1927   31

1927, which again shows that FDR did nothing to stop Japan and its aggressive moves that began in the Pacific. However, first the scholar should also know about the slogan used by the Japanese from 1927 to the end of the Second World War, Hakko Ichiu, and its true meaning that goes hand-in-hand with the Tanaka Memorial.

Hakkō ichiu or Hakkō iu was a Japanese political slogan meaning the divine right of the Empire of Japan to 'unify the eight corners of the world'. It was prominent from the Second Sino-Japanese War to the Second World War, popularised in a speech by Prime Minister of Japan Fumimaro Konoe on 8 January 1940.

Konoe's second cabinet employed the slogan Hakko Ichiu in its July 1940 Outline of Basic National Policies, which spelled out the basic ideas of Japan's war footing and of what came to be called the Greater East Asia Co-Prosperity Sphere. At the outset, it said to the effect that 'the kernel of the national policy is to make the establishment of world peace happen on the basis of the great spirit of the founding of the nation – putting all the corners of the world under one roof – and to build the new order in greater East Asia, in which Imperial Japan serves as the core and strong combination of Japan, Manchukuo and China the root and the trunk.' The slogan Hakko Ichiu, embodying the idea of making one world with Japan headed by the emperor leading other countries, came to be used to justify the Japanese invasion of other countries in the Asia-Pacific region. This was the plan for Japan's world conquest. So to restate, China was in the mist of civil war with Chiang Kai-shek and Mao Tse-tung, and Russia had way too many problems of its own to devise such an amazingly correct document as this; Stalin being too busy in 1937 with the purge to even contemplate such an idea. The other thing that needs to be remembered here is that Young China Publishing managed to get a copy of this document in 1936, which is a year before Stalin supposedly came up with this fraud document. This is a slap in the face of any historian who is studying true history. So yes this is a real, top secret document of the Japanese warlords and Imperial Japanese Army. Some scholars, both Japanese and America, want to say that there has never been any Tanaka Memorial found in the Japanese Archives. Do not forget that the Japanese destroyed thousands upon thousands of documents at the end of the Second World War to protect many of these guilty parties. Even as late as 2006 Japan was trying to cover up its war crimes. Any serious historian or scholar should take anything Japan's government says with a grain of salt. The fact that they honour their war criminals with a shrine, lie about their war crimes in the Second World War, and even teach a false history in their schools is enough to show their retelling of history cannot always be believed so, yes, in the author's opinion the Tanaka Memorial is real.

The Tanaka Memoria
by Tanaka Giichi

Since the European War, Japan's political as well as economic interests have been in an unsettled condition. This is due to the fact that we have failed to take advantage of our special privileges in Manchuria and Mongolia and fully to realize our acquired rights. But upon my appointment as premier, I was instructed to guard our interests in this region and watch for opportunities for further expansion. Such injunctions one cannot take lightly. Ever since I advocated a positive policy toward Manchuria and Mongolia as a common citizen, I have longed for its realization. So in order that we may lay plans for the colonization of the Far East and the development of our new continental empire, a special conference was held from 27 June to 7 July 7th lasting in all eleven days. It was attended by all the civil and military officers connected with Manchuria and Mongolia, whose discussions result in the following resolutions. These we respectfully submit to Your Majesty for consideration.

General Considerations

The term Manchuria and Mongolia includes the provinces Fengtien, Kirin, Heilungkiang and Outer and Inner Mongolia.

It extends an area of 74,000 square miles, having a population of 28,000,000 people. The territory is more than three times as large as our own empire not counting Korea and Formosa, but it is inhabited by only one-third as many people. The attractiveness of the lands does not arise from the scarcity of population alone; its wealth of forestry, minerals and agricultural products is also unrivalled elsewhere in the world. In order to exploit these resources for the perpetuation of our national glory, we created especially the South Manchuria Railway Company. The total investment involved in our undertakings in railway, shipping, mining, forestry, steel manufacture, agriculture, and in cattle raising, as schemes pretending to be mutually beneficial to China and Japan, amount to no less than Yen 440,000,000. It is veritably the largest single investment and the strongest organisation of our country. Although nominally the enterprise is under the joint ownership of the government and the people, in reality it has complete power and authority. In so far as the South Manchuria Railway is empowered to undertake diplomatic, police, and ordinary administrative functions so that it may carry out our imperialistic policies, the Company forms a peculiar organisation which has exactly the same powers as the Governor-General of Korea. This fact alone is sufficient to indicate the immense interests we have in Manchuria and Mongolia. Consequently the policies toward this country of successive administrations since Meiji are all based on his injunctions, elaborating and continuously completing the development of the new continental empire in order to further the advance of our national glory and prosperity for countless generations to come. Unfortunately, since the European War there have been constant changes in diplomatic as well as domestic affairs. The authorities of the Three Eastern Provinces are also awakened and gradually work toward reconstruction and industrial development following our example. Their progress is astonishing. It has affected the spread of our influence in a most serious way, and has put us to so many disadvantages that the dealings with Manchuria and Mongolia of successive governments have resulted in failure. Furthermore, the restrictions of the Nine Power Treaty signed at the Washington Conference have reduced our special rights and privileges in Manchuria and Mongolia to such an extent that there is no freedom left for us. The very existence of our country is endangered. Unless these obstacles are removed, our national existence will be insecure and our national strength will not develop. Moreover, the resources of wealth are congregated in North Manchuria. If we do not have the right of way here, it is obvious that we shall not be able to tap the riches of this country. Even the resources of South Manchuria which we won by the Russo-Japanese War will also be greatly restricted by the Nine Power Treaty. The result is that while our people cannot migrate into Manchuria as they please, the Chinese are flowing in as a flood. Hordes of them move into the Three Eastern Provinces every year, numbering in the neighbourhood of several millions. They have jeopardised our acquired rights in Manchuria and Mongolia to such an extent that our annual surplus population of eight hundred thousand have no place to seek refuge. In view of this we have to admit our failure in trying to effect a balance between our population and food supply. If we do not devise plans to check the influx of Chinese immigrants immediately, in five years' time the number of Chinese will exceed 6,000,000. Then we shall be confronted with greater difficulties in Manchuria and Mongolia. It will be recalled that when the Nine Power Treaty was signed which restricted our movements in Manchuria and Mongolia, public opinion was greatly aroused. The late Emperor Taisho called a conference of Yamagata and other high officers of the army and navy to find a way to counteract this new engagement. I was sent to Europe and America to ascertain secretly the attitude of the important statesmen toward it. They were all agreed that the Nine Power Treaty was initiated by the United States. The other Powers which signed it were willing to see our influence increase in Manchuria and Mongolia in order that we may protect the interests of international trade and investments. This attitude I found out personally from the political leaders of England, France and Italy. The sincerity of these expressions could be depended upon. Unfortunately just as we were ready to carry out our policy and declare void the Nine Power Treaty with the approval of those whom I met on my trip, the Seiyukai cabinet suddenly fell and our policy failed of fruition. It was indeed a great pity. After I had secretly exchanged views with the Powers regarding the development of Manchuria and Mongolia, I returned by way of Shanghai. At the wharf there a Chinese attempted to take my life. An American woman was hurt, but I escaped by the divine protection of my emperors of the past. It seems that it was by divine will that I should assist Your Majesty to open a new era in the Far East and to develop the new continental empire. The Three Eastern Provinces are politically the imperfect spot in the Far East. For the sake of self-protection as well as the protection of others, Japan cannot remove the difficulties in Eastern Asia unless she adopts a policy of Blood and Iron. But in carrying out this policy we have to face the United States which has been turned against us by China's policy of fighting poison with poison. In the future if we want to control China, we must first crush the United States just as in the past we had to fight in the Russo-Japanese War. But in order to conquer China we must first conquer Manchuria and Mongolia. In order to conquer the world, we must first conquer China. If we succeed in conquering China the rest of the Asiatic countries and the South Sea countries will fear us and surrender to us. Then the world will realize that Eastern Asia is ours and will not dare to violate our rights. This is the plan left to us by Emperor

Meiji, the success of which is essential to our national existence. The Nine Power Treaty is entirely an expression of the spirit of commercial rivalry. It was the intention of England and America to crush our influence in China with their power of wealth. The proposed reduction of armaments is nothing but a means to limit our military strength, making it impossible for us to conquer the vast territory of China. On the other hand, China's sources of wealth will be entirely at their disposal. It is merely a scheme by which England and America may defeat our plans. And yet the Minseito made the Nine Power Treaty the important thing and emphasized our TRADE rather than our RIGHTS in China. This is a mistaken policy – a policy of national suicide. England can afford to talk about trade relations only because she has India and Australia to supply her with foodstuffs and other materials. So can America because South America and Canada are there to supply her needs. Their spare energy could be entirely devoted to developing trade in China to enrich themselves. But in Japan her food supply and raw materials decrease in proportion to her population. If we merely hope to develop trade, we shall eventually be defeated by England and America, who possess unsurpassable capitalistic power. In the end, we shall get nothing. A more dangerous factor is the fact that the people of China might someday wake up. Even during these years of internal strife, they can still toil patiently, and try to imitate and displace our goods so as to impair the development of our trade. When we remember that the Chinese are our principal customers, we must beware lest one day when China becomes unified and her industries become prosperous, Americans and Europeans will compete with us; our trade in China will be wrecked. Minseito's proposal to uphold the Nine Power Treaty and to adopt the policy of trade toward Manchuria is nothing less than a suicide policy. After studying the present conditions and possibilities of our country, our best policy lies in the direction of taking positive steps to secure rights and privileges in Manchuria and Mongolia. These will enable us to develop our trade. This will not only forestall China's own industrial development, but also prevent the penetration of European Powers. This is the best policy possible! The way to gain actual rights in Manchuria and Mongolia is to use this region as a base and under the pretence of trade and commerce penetrate the rest of China. Armed by the rights already secured we shall seize the resources all over the country. Having China's entire resources at our disposal we shall proceed to conquer India, the Archipelago, Asia Minor, Central Asia, and even Europe. But to get control of Manchuria and Mongolia is the first step if the Yamato race wish to distinguish themselves on Continental Asia. Final success belongs to the country having food supply; industrial prosperity belongs to the country having raw materials; the full growth of national strength belongs to the country having extensive territory. If we pursue a positive policy to enlarge our rights in Manchuria and China, all these prerequisites of a powerful nation will constitute no problem. Furthermore our surplus population of 700,000 each year will also be taken care of. If we want to inaugurate a new policy and secure the permanent prosperity of our empire, a positive policy toward Manchuria and Mongolia is the only way. Manchuria and Mongolia Not Chinese Territory Historically considered, Manchuria and Mongolia are neither China's territory nor her special possessions. Dr Yano has made an extensive study of Chinese history and has come to the positive conclusion that Manchuria and Mongolia never were Chinese territory. This fact was announced to the world on the authority of the Imperial University. The accuracy of Dr Yano's investigations is such that no scholars in China have contested his statement. However, the most unfortunate thing is that in our declaration of war with Russia our government openly recognised China's sovereignty over these regions and later again at the

Washington Conference when we signed the Nine Power Treaty. Because of these two miscalculations (on our part) China's sovereignty in Manchuria and Mongolia is established in diplomatic relations, but our interests are seriously injured. In the past, although China speaks of the Republic of Five Races, yet Thibet, Sinkiang, Mongolia and Manchuria have always remained special areas and the princes are permitted to discharge their customary functions. Therefore in reality the sovereign power over these regions resides with the princes. When the opportunity presents itself we should make known to the world the actual situation there. We should also wedge our way into Outer and Tanner Mongolia in order that we may reform the mainland. So long as the princes there maintain their former administrations, the sovereign rights are clearly in their hands. If we want to enter these territories, we may regard them as the ruling power and negotiate with them for rights and privileges. We shall be afforded excellent opportunities and our national influence will increase rapidly.

Positive Policy in Manchuria
As to the rights in Manchuria, we should take forceful steps on the basis of the Twenty-One Demands and secure the following in order to safeguard the enjoyment of the rights which we have acquired so far:

1. After the thirty-year commercial lease terminates, we should be able to extend the term at our wish. Also the right of leasing land for commercial, industrial and agricultural purposes should be recognized.
2. Japanese subjects shall have the right to travel and reside in the eastern part of Mongolia, and engage in commercial and industrial activities. As to their movements, China shall allow them freedom from Chinese law. Furthermore,

they must not be subject to illegal taxation and unlawful examination.
3. We must have the right of exploiting the nineteen iron and coal mines in Fengtien and Kirin, as well as the right of timbering.
4. We should have priority for building railroads and option for loans for such purposes in South Manchuria and Eastern Mongolia.
5. The number of Japanese political, financial and military advisers and training officers must be increased. Furthermore, we must have priority in furnishing new advisers.
6. The right of stationing our police over the Koreans (in China).
7. The administration and development of the Kirin Changchun Railway must be extended to 99 years.
8. Exclusive right of sale of special products – priority of shipping business to Europe and America.
9. Exclusive rights of mining in Heilungkiang.
10. Right to construct Kirin-Hueining and Changchun-Talai Railways.
11. In case money is needed for the redemption of the Chinese Eastern Railway, the Japanese Government must have the first option for making loans to China.
12. Harbour rights at Antung and Yingko and the right of through transportation.
13. The right of partnership in establishing a Central Bank of the Three Eastern Provinces.
14. Right of Pasturage. Positive Policy toward Inner and Outer Mongolia since Manchuria and Mongolia are still in the hands of the former princes, in the future we must recognise them as the ruling power and give them support. For this reason, the daughter of General Fukushima, Governor of Kwantung, risked her life among the barbarous Mongolian

people of Tushiyeh to become adviser to their Prince in order that she might serve the Imperial Government. As the wife of the Prince Ruler is the niece of Manchu Prince Su, the relationship between our Government and the Mongolian Prince became very intimate. The princes of Outer and Inner Mongolia have all shown sincere respect for us, especially after we allured them with special benefits and protection. Now there are 19 Japanese retired military officers in the house of the Tushiyeh. We have acquired already monopoly rights for the purchase of wool, for real estate and for mines. Hereafter we shall send secretly more retired officers to live among them. They should wear Chinese clothes in order to escape the attention of the Mukden Government. Scattered in the territory of the Prince, they may engage themselves in farming, herding or dealing in wool. As to the other principalities, we can employ the same method as in Tushiyeh. Everywhere we should station our retired military officers to dominate in the Princes' affairs. After a large number of our people have moved into Outer and Inner Mongolia, we shall then buy lands at one-tenth of their worth and begin to cultivate rice where feasible in order to relieve our shortage of food supply. Where the land is not suitable for rice cultivation we should develop it for cattle-raising and horse-breeding in order to replenish our military needs. The rest of the land could be devoted to the manufacture of canned goods which we may export to Europe and America. The fur and leather will also meet our needs. Once the opportunity comes, Outer and Inner Mongolia will be ours outright. While the sovereign rights are not clearly defined and while the Chinese and Soviet Governments are engaging their attention elsewhere, it is our opportunity to build our influence. Once we have purchased most of the land there, there will be no room for dispute as to whether Mongolia belongs to the Japanese or the Mongolians. Aided by our military prowess, we shall realize our positive policy. In order to carry out this plan, we should appropriate Yen 1,000,000 from the secret funds of the Army Department's budget so that four hundred retired officers disguised as teachers and Chinese citizens may be sent into Outer and Inner Mongolia to mix with the people, to gain the confidence of the Mongolian princes, to acquire from them rights for pasturage and mining and to lay the foundation of our national interests for the next hundred years.

Encouragement and Protection of Korean Immigration
Since the annexation of Korea, we have had very little trouble. But President Wilson's declaration of the self-determination of races after the European War has been like a divine revelation to the suppressed peoples. The Koreans are no exception. The spirit of unrest has permeated the whole country. Both because of the freedom they enjoy in Manchuria due to the incompetent police system and because of the richness of the country, there are now in the Three Eastern Provinces no fewer than 1,000,000 Koreans. The unlooked-for development is fortunate for our country indeed. From a military and economic standpoint, it has greatly strengthened our influence. From another standpoint, it gives new hope for the administration of Koreans.

They will both be the vanguard for the colonization of virgin fields and furnish a link of contact with the Chinese people. On the one hand, we could utilize the naturalized Koreans to purchase land for rice cultivation; on the other, we could extend to them financial aid through the Co-operative Society, the South Manchuria Railway, etc., so that they may serve as the spearhead of our economic penetration. This will give relief to our problem of food supply, as well as open a new field of opportunity for colonization. The Koreans who have become naturalized Chinese are Chinese only in name; they will return to our fold eventually. They are different from those naturalized Japanese in California and South America. They are naturalized as Chinese only for temporary convenience. When their numbers reach two and a half million or more, they can be instigated to military activities whenever there is the necessity, and under the pretence of suppressing the Koreans we could bear them aid. As not all the Koreans are naturalized Chinese, the world will not be able to tell whether it is the Chinese Koreans or the Japanese Koreans who create the trouble. We can always sell dog's meat with a sheep's head as a signboard. Of course while we could use the Koreans for such purposes, we must beware of the fact that the Chinese could also use them against us. But Manchuria is as much under our jurisdiction as under Chinese jurisdiction. If the Chinese should use Koreans to hamper us, then our opportunity of war against China is at hand. In that event, the most formidable factor is Soviet Russia. If the Chinese should use the 'Reds' to influence the Koreans, the thought of our people will change and great peril will befall us. Therefore, the present Cabinet is taking every precaution against this eventuality. If we want to make use of the Koreans to develop our new continental empire, our protection and regulations for them must be more carefully worked out. We should increase our police force in North Manchuria under the terms of the Mitsuya Treaty so that we may protect the Koreans and give them help in their rapid advance. Furthermore, the Eastern Development Company (Totuku Kaisha) and the South Manchuria Railway Company should follow then to give them financial aid. They should be given especially favourable terms so that through them we may develop Manchuria and Mongolia and monopolise the commercial rights. The influx of Koreans into these territories is of such obvious importance both for economic and military considerations that the Imperial Government cannot afford not to give it encouragement. It will mean new opportunities for our empire. Since the effect of the Lansing-Ishii Agreement is lost after the Washington Conference, we can only recover our interests through the favourable development arising out of the presence of several millions of Koreans in Manchuria. There is no ground in international relations for raising any objection to this procedure. Railroads and Development of Our New Continent Transportation is the mother of the national defense, the assurance of victory and the citadel of economic development. China has only 7,200 to 7,300 miles of railroads, of which three thousand miles are in Manchuria and Mongolia, constituting two-fifths of the whole. Considering the size of Manchuria and Mongolia and the abundance of natural products, there should be at least five or six thousand miles more. It is a pity that our railroads are mostly in South Manchuria, which cannot reach the sources of wealth in the northern parts. Moreover, there are too many Chinese inhabitants in South Manchuria to be wholesome for our military and economic plans. If we wish to develop the natural resources and strengthen our national defense, we must build railroads in Northern Manchuria. With the opening of these railroads, we shall be able to send more people (Japanese) into Northern Manchuria. From this vantage ground we can manipulate political and economic developments in South Manchuria, as well as strengthen our national defense in the interest of peace and order of the Far East. Furthermore, the South Manchuria was built mainly for economic purposes. It lacks encircling lines necessary for military mobilization and transportation. From now on we must take military purposes as our object and build circuit lines to circle the heart of Manchuria and Mongolia in order that we may hamper China's military, political and economic developments there on the one hand, and prevent the penetration of Russian influence on the other. This is the key to our continental policy. There are two trunk lines in Manchuria and Mongolia. These are the Chinese Eastern Railway and the South Manchuria Railway. As regards the railroad built by the Chinese, it will doubtless become very powerful in time, backed by the financial resources of the Kirin Provincial Government. With the combined resources of Fengtien and Heilung-kiang Provinces, the Chinese railroads will develop to an extent far superior to our South Manchuria Railway. Strong competition will inevitably result. Fortunately for us, the financial conditions in Fengtien Province are in great disorder, which the authorities cannot improve unless we come to their aid. This is our chance. We should take positive steps until we have reached our goal in railroad development. Moreover, if we manipulate the situation, the Fengtien bank notes will depreciate to an inconceivable degree. In that event, the bankruptcy of Fengtien will be a matter of time. The development of Manchuria and Mongolia will be out of the question for them. But we still have to reckon with the Chinese Eastern Railway. It forms a T with the South Manchuria Railway. Although this system is a convenient shape, it is by no means suitable for military purposes. When the Chinese build railroads as feeders of the Chinese Eastern Railway, it is best that they run parallel to it, west and east. But with the South Manchuria Railway as main line, we must have these lines run north and south. For the benefit of the Chinese themselves, there are also advantages for these lines to run in this direction. Consequently our interest does not necessarily conflict with the Chinese. Now that Russia is losing influence and is powerless to advance in Manchuria and Mongolia, it is certain that the Chinese must act according to our reckoning in the development of railways in the future. Much to our surprise the Fengtien Government recently built two railroads, one from Tahushan to Tungliao and the other from Kirin to Haining, both for military purposes. These two rail-roads affect most seriously our military plans in Manchuria and Mongolia as well as the interest of the South Manchuria Railway. We therefore protested strongly against it. That these railways were built was due to the fact that our official on the spot as well as the South Manchuria Railway authorities miscalculated the ability of the Fengtien Government and paid no attention to it. Later when we did intervene the railways were already completed. Besides, the Americans have been anxious to make an investment in developing the port of Hu-lu-tao through British capitalists. Taking advantage of this situation, the Fengtien Government introduced American and British capital in these railways in order to hold our interest at bay. For the time being we have to wink at it and wait for the opportune moment to deal with China about these two railroads. Recently, it is rumored, that the Fengtien Government is planning to build a railroad from Tahushan to Harbin via Tung Liao and Fu Yu, so that there may be a direct line between Peking and Harbin without touching either the South Manchuria Railway or the Chinese Eastern Railway. What is more astonishing is that another railway beginning at Mukden passing through Hailung, Kirin, Wuchang and terminating at Harbin is also under way. If this plan becomes true, then these two lines would encircle the South Manchuria Railway and limit its sphere of activities to a small area. The result is that our economic and political development of Manchuria and Mongolia will be checked and the plan for curtailing our power by the Nine Power Treaty will be carried out. Moreover, the completion of these two railroads will render the South Manchuria Railway completely useless. The latter company will be confronted with a real crisis. But in view of China's financial conditions to-day, she cannot undertake these two railroads unless she resorts to foreign loans. And on these two railways the transportation charges will have to be higher than on the South Manchuria Railway. These considerations give us some comfort. But in the event of these two railroads becoming an accomplished fact and the Chinese Government making especially low freight charges in order to compete with the South Manchuria Railway, not only we but the Chinese Eastern Railway will also sustain great losses. Japan and Russia certainly would not allow China to carry out such obstructive measures, especially as the Chinese Eastern Railway depends upon Tsitsihar and Harbin for the bulk of its business. The consequence would be even more serious to both Japanese and Russian interests when the new railways are completed.

Let us consider more in detail the competitive railways projected in Manchuria and Mongolia. China contemplates: 1. Suolun-Taonan Railway. 2. Kirin-Harbin Railway. Soviet Russia proposes: 1. Anta-Potung Railway. 2. Mienpo-Wuchang-Potuna Railway. 3. Kirin-Hailin Railway. 4. Mishan-Muling Railway. The Russian plans are designed to strengthen the Chinese Eastern Railway and thereby to extend its imperialistic schemes. For this reason the railways projected mostly run east and west. For although the power of Soviet Russia is declining, her ambition in Manchuria and Mongolia has not diminished for a minute. Every step she takes is intended to obstruct our progress and to injure the South Manchuria Railway. We must do our utmost to guard against her influence. We should use the Fengtien

Government as a wedge to check her southern advance. By pretending to check the southern advance of Soviet Russia as a first step, we could gradually force our way into North Manchuria and exploit the natural resources there. We shall then be able to prevent the spread of Chinese influence on the south and arrest the advance of Soviet Russia on the north. In our struggle against the political and economic influence of Soviet Russia, we should drive China before us and direct the event from behind. Meanwhile, we should still secretly befriend Russia in order to hamper the growth of Chinese influence. It was largely with this purpose in view that Baron Goto of Kato's cabinet invited Joffe to our country and advocated the resumption of diplomatic relations with Russia. Although we have an agreement with the Chinese Eastern Railway concerning transportation rates, according to which 45 per cent go to the Chinese Eastern Railway and 55 per cent to us, yet the Chinese Eastern Railway still grants preferential rates detrimental to the interest of the South Manchuria Railway. Moreover, according to a secret declaration of Soviet Russia, although they have no territorial ambition they cannot help keeping a hand in the Chinese Eastern Railway on account of the fact that north of the Chinese and Russian boundary the severe cold makes a railway valueless. Furthermore, as Vladivostok is their only seaport in the Far East, they cannot give up the Chinese Eastern Railway without losing also their foothold on the Pacific. This makes us feel the more uneasy. On the other hand the South Manchuria Railway is not adequate for our purpose. Considering our present needs and future activities, we must control railways in both north and south Manchuria, especially in view of the fact that the resources of North Manchuria and Eastern Mongolia will furnish no room for expansion and material gains. In South Manchuria the Chinese are increasing at such a rate that it surely will damage our interests politically and economically. Under such circumstances, we are compelled to take aggressive steps in North Manchuria in order to assure our future prosperity. But if the Chinese Eastern Railway of Soviet Russia should spread across this field our new continental policy is bound to receive a setback which will result in an inevitable conflict with Soviet Russia in the near future. In that event we shall enact once more our part in the Russo-Japanese War. The Chinese Eastern Railway will become ours as the South Manchuria Railway did last time, and we shall seize Kirin as we once did Dairen. That we should draw swords with Russia again in the fields of Mongolia in order to gain the wealth of North Manchuria seems a necessary step in our programmed of national aggrandizement. Until this hidden rock is blown up our ship cannot have smooth sailing. We should now demand from China the right of building all the important military railroads. When these railroads are completed, we shall pour our forces into North Manchuria as far as we can. When Soviet Russia intervenes, as they must, that is our opportunity for open conflict. We should insist on the building of the following railways:

1. Tungliao-Jehol Railway. This line is 447 miles long and will cost Yen 1,000,000. When it is completed it will be of great value to our development of Inner Mongolia. As a matter of fact, this is the most important of all the railways in the whole undertaking. According to the careful surveys of the War Department, there are in Inner Mongolia large tracts of land suitable for rice cultivation. After proper development there will be room for at least 20 millions of our people. There is besides the possibility of turning out 2,000,000 head of cattle which may be transported by

railways for food supply and for purposes of exporting to Europe and America. Wool also is a special product. While the sheep in Japan yield only two catties of wool per head per year, the sheep in Mongolia can yield six catties. The South Manchuria Railway has made many experiments, all of which confirm this fact. Besides, the wool is many times better than that of Australia. Its low cost and high quality combined with its abundance in quantity make Mongolia a potential source of great wealth. When this industry is enhanced by the facilities of railway development, the total production will increase at least ten-fold. We have withheld this knowledge from the rest of the world, lest England and America compete with us for it. Therefore, we must first of all control the transportation and then develop the wool industry. By the time the other countries know about it, it would be already too late to do anything. With this railroad in our hands, we can develop the wool industry not only for our own use, but also for exporting to Europe and America. Furthermore, we can realize our desire of joining hands with Mongolia. This railway is a matter of life and death to our policy in Mongolia. Without it, Japan can have no part in Mongolia's development.

2. Suolun-Taonan Railway. This line is 136 miles long and will cost Yen 10,000,000. Looking into the future of Japan, a war with Russia over the plains of North Manchuria is inevitable. From a military standpoint, this line will not only enable us to threaten Russia's rear, but also to curtail its reinforcements for North Manchuria. From an economic standpoint, this road will place the wealth of the Tao-er-ho Valley within our reach, thereby strengthening the South Manchuria Railway. The princes nearby who are friendly to us can also use this road to extend our influence in order to open up their respective territories. Our hope of working

hand in hand with the Mongolian princes, of acquiring land, mines and pasturage, and of developing trade with the natives as preliminary steps for later penetration, all depend upon this railway. Together with the Tungliao-Jehol Railway, they will form two supplementary routes into Mongolia. When the industries are fully developed, we shall extend our interests into Outer Mongolia. But the danger of this line is that it might provide facilities for Chinese migration into a new region and spoil our policy. Look at our experience with the South Manchuria Railway. Hasn't that served the interest of China? The redeeming feature, however, is the fact that the land and mines along this railway are in the possession of Mongolian princes. If we can gain possession of them first, we need have no worries about Chinese migration. Moreover, we can make the princes pass laws discriminating against Chinese immigrants. When life there is made miserable for the Chinese, they naturally will leave for places afar. There are other methods to bar the Chinese. Only if we try hard enough, no Chinese footprints will be found on Mongolian territory.

3. A section of the Changchun-Taonan Railway. As this line runs from Changchun to Fuyu and Talai, the section between Changchun and Taonan is about 131 miles and costs approximately 1,000,000 Yen. This line is immensely important from an economic standpoint, for the wealth of Manchuria and Mongolia lies all in North Manchuria. It will enable us to have an easy access to North Manchuria on the one hand, and prejudice the Chinese Eastern Railway to the benefit of the South Manchuria Railway on the other. It runs through the upper valley of the Sungari River where the soil is fertile and agricultural products abound. Further, in the vicinity of Talai there is the Yueh-Liang Falls which

could be harnessed for electric power. That this section of the railway will be a prosperous centre for industry and agriculture is beyond doubt. After the completion of this line, we shall be able to make Talai a base and advance on Siberia through three directions; namely, by way of Taonan, Anshan and Tsitsihar. The wealth of North Manchuria will then come to our hands. This will also be the first line of advance to Heilungkiang. It will further form a circuit with the railway between Changchun and Taonan, which will serve well for military purposes when we penetrate into Mongolia. Along this whole line the population is sparse and the land is rich and extensive. No fertilizer will be required on the farms for fifty years. A possession of this railway will ensure the possession of all the wealth of North Manchuria and Mongolia. In this region there is room for at least 30 million people more. When the Tunhua Railway is completed and joins up with the line running to Hueining in Korea, the products will be brought to the door of Osaka and Tokyo by a direct route. In time of war our troops could be dispatched to North Manchuria and Mongolia via the Japan Sea without a stop, forestalling all possibilities of Chinese forces entering North Manchuria. Nor could American or Russian submarines enter the Korean Strait. The moment the railways between Kirin and Hueining and between Changchun and Talai are completed, we shall become self-sufficient in foodstuffs and raw materials. We shall have no worries in the event of war with any country. Then, in our negotiation with Manchuria and Mongolia, China will be cowed to submission and yield to our wishes. If we want to end the political existence of Manchuria and Mongolia according to the third step of Meiji's plan, the completion of these two railways is the only way. The Changchun-Talai Railway will greatly enhance the value of the South

Manchuria Railway, besides developing into a profitable line itself. It is an undertaking of supreme importance in our penetration into this territory.

4. The Kirin-Hueining Line. While the Kirin-Tunhua Line is already completed, the Tunhua-Hueining Line is yet to be built. The narrow gauge of 2 ft 6 inches of the track from Hueining to Laotoukow is inadequate for the economic development of the New Continent. Allowing Yen 8,000,000 for widening the tracks in this section and Yen 10,000,000 for completing the section between Laotoukow and Tunhua, the whole undertaking will cost approximately Yen 20,000,000. When this is done, our continental policy will have succeeded. Hitherto, people going to Europe have to pass through either Dairen or Vladivostok. Now they can go on the trunk line directly from Chingchinkwang via the Siberian Railway. When we are in control of this great system of transportation, we need make no secret of our designs on Manchuria or Mongolia according to the third step of Meiji's plans. The Yamato Race is then embarked on the journey of world conquest! According to the last will of Meiji, our first step was to conquer Formosa and the second step to annex Korea. Having completed both of these, the third step is yet to be taken and that is the conquest of Manchuria, Mongolia and China. When this is done, the rest of Asia including the South Sea Islands will be at our feet. That these injunctions have not been carried out even now, is a crime of your humble servants. In history the people living in Kirin, Fengtien and part of Heilungkiang, are called Sushan. They are now scattered along the sea coast and in the basins of the Amur and Tumen rivers. They were known as Kulai, Sushan, Hueibei, Palou, Wotsu, Fuyu, Kitan, Pohai and Nuchen at different stages of history. They were of a mixed race. The forefathers of

the Manchurian dynasty also began in this vicinity. They gained control of Kirin, first, and then firmly established themselves in China for 300 years. If we want to put into effect our Continental Policy, we have to note this historical fact and proceed to establish ourselves in this region first also. Hence the necessity of the Kirin-Hueining Railway. Whether the terminus of the Kirin-Hueining Line be at Chingchu or Lochin or even Hsiungchi, we are free to decide according to circumstances. From the standpoint of national defence at present Lochin seems the ideal and terminus. Eventually it will be the best in the world. On the one hand it will ruin Vladivostok, and on the other it will be the centre of the wealth of Manchuria and Mongolia. Moreover, Dairen is as yet not our own territory. While Manchuria is yet not a part of our empire, it is difficult to develop Dairen. That being the case, we shall be in a precarious situation in time of war. The enemy could blockade the Tsushima and Senchima straits, and we would be cut off from the supplies of Manchuria and Mongolia. Not having the resources there at our command we would be vanquished, especially as England and the United States have worked hand in hand to limit our action in every possible direction. For the sake of self-preservation and of giving warning to China and the rest of the world, we must fight America some time. The American Asiatic Squadron stationed in the Philippines is but within a stone's throw from Tsushima and Senchima. If they send submarines to these quarters, our supply of foodstuffs and raw materials from Manchuria and Mongolia will be cut off entirely. But if the Kirin-Hueining Railway is completed, we shall have a large circuit line through all Manchuria and Korea, and a small circuit line through North Manchuria. We shall have access in all directions gaining freedom for the transportation of soldiers and supplies alike. When our supplies are transported through this line to our ports at Tsuruga and Niigata, enemy submarines will have no way of getting into the Japanese and Korean straits. We are then entirely free from interference. This is what is meant by making the Japanese Sea the centre of our national defense. Having secured the free transportation of food and raw materials, we shall have nothing to fear either from the American navy because of its size, or the Chinese or Russian army because of their number. Incidentally, we shall be in a position to suppress the Koreans. Let me reiterate the fact that if we want to carry out the New Continental Policy, we must build this line. Manchuria and Mongolia are the undeveloped countries in the East. Over this territory we shall have to go to war with Soviet Russia sooner or later. The battleground will be in Kirin. When we carry out the third step of Meiji's plans with regard to China, we shall have to do the following things:

1. Mobilize the army divisions in Fukuoka and Hiroshima, and send them to South Manchuria via Korea. This will prevent the northern advance of Chinese soldiers.

2. Send the army divisions in Nagoya and Kwansei by sea to Ghingchin, and thence to North Manchuria via the Kirin-Hueining Line.

3. Send the army in Kwantung through Niigata to Chingchin or Lochin, and thence by Kirin-Hueining Line to North Manchuria.

4. Send the army divisions in Hokkaido and Sendai to embark the ship at Aomori and Hakodato, and sail for Vladivostok; thence via the Siberian Railway to Harbin. Then they can descend on Fengtien, seize Mongolia and prevent Russian forces from coming south.

5. Finally these divisions in all directions will meet and form themselves into two large armies. On the south, they will

keep Shanhaikwan and close it against the northern advance of Chinese forces; on the north, they will defend Tsitsihar against the southern advance of the Russians. In this way we shall have all the resources of Manchuria and Mongolia at our command. Even if the war should be prolonged for ten years, we need have no fear for the lack of supplies.

Let us now analyze once more the Kirin-Hueining Railway from the standpoint of its access from our ports. First with Chingchin as the starting point:

1. To Vladivostok – 130 miles.
2. To Tsuruga – 475 miles.
3. To Moji – 500 miles.
4. To Nagasaki – 650 miles.
5. To Fushun – 500 miles.

Second, take Tsuruga as the port of entry and compare it with Dairen. In this case we should consider it from the point of view of Osaka as industrial centre.

1. From Changchun to Osaka via Lochin, the distance is 406 miles by land and 475 miles by sea. In point of time the route will take 51 hours.
2. From Changchun to Osaka via Dairen and Kobe, the distance is 535 miles by land and 870 miles by sea. In point of time it takes 92 hours. If Tsuruga instead of Dairen is made the connecting link, there is a saving of 41 hours. Calculated at the rate of 30 miles an hour on land and 12 miles an hour by sea, we can use fast boats and trains and cut the time in half. Manchuria and Mongolia are the Belgium of the Far East. In the Great War, Belgium was the battlefield. In our wars with Russia and the United States, we must also make Manchuria and Mongolia suffer the ravages. As it is evident that we have to violate the neutrality of these territories, we cannot help building the Kirin-Hueining and Changchun-Talai Railways in order that we may be militarily prepared. In time of war

we can easily increase our forces and in time of peace we can migrate thousands upon thousands of people into this region and work on the rice fields. This line offers the key to economic development as well as to military conquests. In undertaking the Kirin-Hueining Railway, it is necessary to take advantage of the dry season and finish it at one stretch. The mountains we must go through are all granite. This would need modern and up-to-date machines. As to the sleepers and ballast required, there is an abundance all along the line. Limestone and clay for making tiles and brick are also to be had for the taking. Only rails, cars and locomotives have to be brought in. The cost of construction could therefore be reduced at least 30 per cent and the time required 40 per cent. Now let us look into the economic interests along this line. According to the careful investigation of our General Staff and the South Manchuria Railway, the total reserve of timber is 200,000,000 tons. If one million tons is felled and imported to our country each year, it will last two hundred years. This will stop the imports of American timber which has been costing us Yen 80,000,000 to Yen 100,000,000 a year. Although our information is reliable we cannot make it known to the world; for if China or Russia learns that we get so much timber from America, they would try to interfere with the construction of this line. Or else, the United States may buy from the Fengtien Government all the timber rights on the one hand to protect their own trade with us; on the other, to control the monopoly and incidentally kill our paper industry. Kirin was known as the 'ocean of trees' even in the days of Emperor Chien-Lung. Added to the original forests are the growths in the intervening years since that time. Imagine the vastness of the resources! To transport this timber from Kirin to Osaka via Changchun and Dairen, there is a distance of 1,385 miles. For every cubic foot, we have to spend 34 cents. Because of this high cost of transportation, we cannot compete with the United States. If the Kirin-Hueining Line is completed, the distance is reduced to about 700 miles. We can then ship timber to Osaka at the low rate of 13 cents per cubic foot. We can certainly defeat the timber from the United States then. Supposing we calculate the profit at Yen 5.00 per ton of timber and supposing there are two billion tons of timber, the construction of the railway will bring to us the easy profit of 10 million yen. Besides, we will bar the import of American timber into our country. Furthermore, the industry of furniture making, paper manufacture and other usages which the cheap timber makes possible will add 20 million yen more to our country's annual income. There is also the Hsin Chin coal mine, which has a reserve of 600,000,000 tons of coal. The quality of this coal is superior to that of Fushun coal, easy to excavate and suitable for the extraction of petroleum, agricultural fertilizers and other chemical by-products which we may both use at home and sell in China. There are numerous other advantages which will come to us from the building of the Kirin-Hueining Railway. It is all gain without labor. The coal will supplement the Fushun colliers. With both coal mines in our control, we hold the key to the industries of all China. Speaking of the Hsin Chin coal, we shall reap a profit of Yen 5.00 on each ton when it is shipped to Japan. With additional chemical by-products, we shall reap a profit of Yen 16.00 from each ton of coal. Taking an average profit of Yen 15.00 a ton, the total profit will amount to 200 billion yen. All this comes as a by-product from the operation of the Kirin-Hueining Railway. There are, besides, the gold mines along the Mutan River. The acquired rights of the South Manchuria Railway in the gold mines of Chia-Pikou in the province of Kirin and the timber in the neighbourhood will all be within reach of exploitation once the Kirin-Hueining line is in operation. In the vicinity of Tunhua, the agricultural products, such as oats, wheat, millet and Koaliang, yield an annual output of over a million catties. There are twenty distilleries of wines, thirty oil mills yielding an annual output of about 600,000 catties of oil and 600,000 of bean cakes, besides many other places for making vermicelli. All these will depend upon the new railway. The trade along this road may be estimated at four million yen a year. The transportation charges of farm products alone will not only defray the running expenses, but also yield a net profit of Yen 200,000 per year. Including the net profit from timber, coal and its by-products transported by the railways, we can safely count on a profit of Yen 8,000,000 a year. Besides, there are indirect benefits such as strengthening of the South Manchuria Railway, the acquisition of rights over forests, mines and trade as well as the migration of large numbers of our people into North Manchuria. Above all, is the shortening of distance between Japan and the resources of wealth in North Manchuria. It takes only three hours from Chingchin to Hueining, three hours from Hueining to Sanfeng and three hours more from Tumen River to Lung-Ching-Tsun. In 60 hours we can reach the wealth of North Manchuria. Hence the Kirin-Hueining Railroad alone can enable us to tap the immense wealth of North Manchuria.

3. Hunchun-Hailin Railway. This is 173 miles long and cost Yen 24,000,000. All along this line are thick forests. In order to strengthen the Kirin-Hueining Railway and to exploit the forests and mines in North Manchuria, this line is needed. In order to transfer the prosperity of Vladivostok to Hueining, this line is also urgently needed. The greatest hope for prosperity, however, is the fact that south of Naining and north of Tunhua there is Lake Chingpo which

can be used to generate electric power. With this electric power, we shall have control over the agricultural and industrial undertakings of the whole of Manchuria and Mongolia. No amount of Chinese agitation can matter in the least to our industrial developments. According to the investigations of the South Manchuria Railway, the water power in the lake can generate at least 800,000 horse-power. With such an enormous quantity of electric power, the industrial conquest of Manchuria and Mongolia can be easily accomplished. In the neighborhood of this immense power plant, there will be phenomenal growth of wealth. We must build this railway quickly, in order to provide facilities for transportation. Lake Hsing Kai, which is owned jointly by China and Russia, can also be developed for the generation of electricity. In order that these two countries may not combine to frustrate our plans, we should introduce a resolution in the International Conference of Electrical Engineering to be held in Tokyo this year, to the effect that in the same area of electricity supply there should not be two power plants. Besides, in the vicinity of Niigata and Hailin, the Oju Paper Mill has acquired extensive rights of lumbering. They need the immediate establishment of the power plant at Lake Chingpo and the early completion of the Hunchun-Hailin Railway in order to bring to the factory at home the raw materials growing wild in Mongolia. Moreover, the reason that the Feng-Kirin-Wuchang Railway and the Kirin-tien authorities intend to build the Wuchang Railway and the Kirin Mukden Railway, with Hulutao or Tientsin as seaport, is that they want to recover to themselves the wealth of North Manchuria. By building the Hunchun-Hailin Railway we shall not only strengthen the Kirin-Hueining Railway, but also defeat the Chinese scheme and draw the wealth of Manchuria to Chingchin Harbor. The transportation charges will be two-thirds less compared with the Chinese line and one-third less compared with the Siberian line. They cannot compete with us. Our victory is a foregone conclusion. The total trade in Manchuria is seven or eight billion yen a year, all of which is in our hands. The business we do in wool, cotton, soy beans, bean cakes and iron, forms one-twentieth of the total volume of world trade. And it is steadily increasing. But the Namihaya Machi at Dairen (the wealthiest street in the city) is still in Chinese possession. The sad story goes further. Oil is a basic industry in Manchuria. We control only 6 per cent of it. Of the 38 oil mills in Yingkow there is not one Japanese; of the 20 oil mills in Antung there is only one Japanese and of the 82 or 83 oil mills in Dairen there are only seven owned by Japanese. This is by no means an optimistic outlook for us. In order to recover the lost ground, we must first of all develop transportation. Then, by securing a monopoly on both finished products and raw materials, we shall be able to gain the upper hand eventually. Furthermore, we ought to assist our people in oil business by extending to them financial credit, so that the oil industry of the Chinese will be forced out of the market. There are many Chinese on Kawaguchi Machi in Osaka who are dealers of our manufactured goods in Mongolia and Manchuria. They are strong competitors of our own business men in China. Our people are greatly handicapped because of their high standard of living which compels them to figure at a higher percentage of profit. On the other hand, the Chinese also have their disadvantages. The goods that they get are of an inferior quality, but the price that they pay is at least 10 per cent higher than what our own people pay. Besides, they are also obliged to pay Yen 2.70 more than our people for every ton of goods transported, and yet they can undersell our merchants in Manchuria. It clearly shows the inability of our own people. When one thinks of it, it is really pathetic. The Chinese is single-handed, receiving no assistance from the government. But the Japanese in Manchuria has every protection from the government and long-term credit at a low rate of interest. Still there are innumerable cases of failures. Hereafter, we should organise a co-operative exporting house to China. The steamship lines and the South Manchuria Railway should give it special discounts, and the government in Kwantung should extend to it financial credit at a very low rate of interest. Then we can hope to beat the Chinese merchants and recover our trade rights, so that we may develop the special products of Manchuria and send them to all parts of the world. The first step in gaining financial and commercial control of Manchuria and Mongolia lies in the monopoly sale of their products. We must have the rights of monopoly for the sale of Manchurian and Mongolian products before we can carry out our Continental Policy and prevent the invasion of American capital as well as the influence of the Chinese traders. Although the products of Manchuria and Mongolia may go through any of the three ports, Dairen, Yingko and Antung, nevertheless Dairen holds the key to the situation. Every year 7,200 ships pass through this port with a total tonnage of 11,565,000 tons. This represents 70 per cent of the total trade of Manchuria and Mongolia. Fifteen navigation routes radiate out from it with definite sailing schedule. Most of it is coastal sailing. We have in our grasp the entire transportation system of Manchuria and Mongolia. The monopoly sale of Manchuria's special products will eventually come into our hands. When that comes true, we can develop our oceanic transportation in order to defeat both Yingko and Antung. Then the large quantities of beans which the central and southern parts of

China consume, will depend upon us entirely. Moreover, the Chinese are an oil-eating people. In time of war, we can cut off their oil supply and the life of the whole country will become miserable. Bean cakes are important as fertilizers for the cultivation of rice. If we have control of the source of supply as well as the means of transportation, we shall be able to increase our production of rice by means of a cheap supply of bean cakes and the fertilizers manufactured as a by-product at the Fushun coal mines. In this way, we shall have the agricultural work of all China dependent upon us. In case of war, we can put an embargo on bean cakes as well as the mineral fertilizers and forbid their exportation to Central and South China. Then China's production of foodstuffs will be greatly reduced. This is one way of building up our continental empire which we must not overlook. We should remember that Europe and America also need large quantities of beans and bean cakes. When we have a monopoly of the supplies and full control of transportation, both on land and sea, the countries which have need of the special products of Manchuria and Mongolia will have to seek our good-will. In order to gain trade monopoly in Manchuria and Mongolia, we must have control of the complete transportation system. Only then can we have the Chinese merchants under our thumb. However, the Chinese are adept in learning our tricks and beating us at our own game. We have yet found no way by which we can compete successfully with them in oil making and sail-boat transportation. After building up the new system of transportation, our policy should be two-fold. On the one hand, wreck the sail-boat trade by means of heavy investment in our own system. On the other hand, encourage our men to learn all they can from the Chinese sail-boat business. Another thing we should be careful about is teaching the Chinese our industrial methods. In the past we have established factories in Manchuria and Mongolia, and carried on industries near the source of raw materials. This gave to the Chinese the opportunity of learning our secrets and establishing competitive factories of their own. Hereafter, we should ship the raw materials back home and do the manufacturing there, and then ship the finished products for sale in China and other countries. In this way we shall gain in three ways: (1) provide work for our unemployed at home; (2) prevent the influx of Chinese into Manchuria and Mongolia, and (3) make it impossible for the Chinese to imitate our new industrial methods. Then iron of Penhsihu and Anshan and the coal of Fushun should also be sent home to be turned into finished products. For all these considerations, the development of ocean transportation becomes the more necessary. The Dairen Kisen Kaisha Company should be enlarged, and our government should extend to it loans at low interest through the South Manchuria Railway Company. By next year we should complete 500,000 tons of new ships for oceanic transportation. That will be sufficient to dominate over the traffic of the East. For on the one hand we have the South Manchuria Railway for land transportation; on the other hand, we control the large quantities of products in Manchuria and Mongolia waiting to be transported. The success of this enlarged activity in oceanic transportation with Dairen as centre is assured by the iron laws of economics. Gold Standard Currency Necessary Although Manchuria and Mongolia are within our field of activities, yet the legal tender there is still silver. It often conflicts with our gold basis and work's to our disadvantage. That our people have failed to prosper as they should in these places is due to the existence of the silver monetary system there.

The Chinese have persistently upheld the silver basis, and therefore have made it impossible for us firmly to establish our colonization plans on a firm economic foundation. We have suffered from it the following disadvantages:

1. The money that we bring into Manchuria is of gold standard. When we use it either for daily livelihood or for industry and trade, it has to be exchanged into Chinese silver dollars. The fluctuation of exchange is not infrequently as much as 20 per cent, resulting in serious loss to our people. Speculation becomes a regular business and investing money becomes a matter of gambling. When one plans an investment of two hundred thousand yen, one may suddenly find that his capital has been reduced to one hundred fifty or one hundred sixty thousand dollars due to the drop in exchange. The creditor would then have to call in the loans and business failures have often resulted.

2. The Chinese business men use silver money throughout and are free from the effects of the exchange fluctuations. Therefore their 'junk' trade is prosperous. Although they have no scientific knowledge of the exchange value of gold and silver, they always gain in the transaction. They have a natural gift for it; we suffer the more. And we lose in spite of our control of the transaction and special backing of banking houses. Because of the handicap of the monetary system, people in Central and South China always buy beans and bean cakes from their own people. We have no chance against them. In consequence, we cannot conquer the whole of China.

3. With the silver standard in existence, the Chinese Government can increase their notes to counteract our gold notes. Consequently our banks will fail to carry out the mission of extending our country's influence.

4. If the gold standard is adopted, we can issue gold notes freely. With the credit of the gold notes, we can acquire

rights in real property and natural resources and defeat the credit of the Chinese silver notes. The Chinese will be unable to compete with us; and the currency of the whole of Manchuria and Mongolia will be in our control.

5. The Government Bank of the Three Eastern Provinces, the Bank of Communications, the Frontier Development Bank and the General Credit and Finance Corporation have in circulation silver notes amounting to $38,000,000. Their reserve funds in the form of buildings and goods are estimated at $1,350,000. It is natural that the Chinese notes should depreciate. It is only by acts of the Government that these notes are still in circulation. Until we have entirely discredited the Chinese silver notes, we will never place our gold notes in their proper place in Manchuria and Mongolia, much less obtain the monopoly in currency and finance of these two countries. With the depreciated and inconvertible silver notes, the government of the Three Eastern Provinces buys all kinds of products, thus threatening our vested interests. When they sell these products, they demand gold from us which they keep for the purpose of wrecking our financial interests including our trade rights in special products. For these reasons, our gold notes are having a harder time and a gold standard for currency becomes the more urgently necessary. In view of the above-mentioned considerations, we must overthrow Manchuria's inconvertible silver notes and divest the government of its purchasing power. Then we can extend the use of our gold notes in the hope of dominating the economic and financial activities of Manchuria and Mongolia. Furthermore, we can compel the authorities of the Three Eastern Provinces to employ Japanese financial advisers to help us gain supremacy in financial matters. When the Chinese notes are overthrown, our gold notes will take their place.

Encourage Investment from a Third Power

It has been our traditional policy to exclude from Manchuria and Mongolia investments of a third power. But since the Nine Power Treaty is based on the principle of equal opportunity for all, the underlying principle of the International Consortium which regards Manchuria and Mongolia as outside its sphere becomes anachronistic. We are constantly under the watchful eyes of the Powers, and every step that we take arouses suspicion. This being the case, we had better invite foreign investments in such enterprises as the development of electric power or the manufacture of alkali. By using American and European capital, we can further our plans for the development of Manchuria and Mongolia. By so doing, we shall allay international suspicion and clear the way for larger plans on the one hand and induce the Powers to recognize the fact of our special position in that country on the other. We should welcome any power wishing to make investment, but we must not allow China to deal with the leading countries at her will. As we are anxious that the Powers recognize the fact of our special position in Manchuria and Mongolia in political as well as economic affairs, we are obliged to intervene and share all responsibilities with her. To make this a customary practice in our diplomatic dealings, is another important policy for us.

The Necessity of Changing the Organization of the South Manchuria Railway

The South Manchuria Railway Company functions in Manchuria as the Governor-General of Korea did there before the annexation. In order to build up our new Continental Empire, we must change the organization of that Company so as to break away from the present difficulties. The functions of this Company are varied and important. Every change of cabinet involves a change of the administration of the South

Manchuria Railway, and conversely every activity of the South Manchuria Railway also has important consequences on the cabinet. This is because the South Manchuria Railway is semi-governmental, with final authority resting in the cabinet. For this reason, the Powers invariably look upon this railway as a purely political organ rather than a business enterprise. Whenever a new move is made for the development of Manchuria and Mongolia, the Powers would invoke the Nine Power Treaty to thwart the plans of the South Manchuria Railway. This has greatly damaged the interests of our empire. Considered from the point of view of domestic administration, the South Manchuria Railway is subject to a quadruple control. There are the Governor of Kwantung, the Chief Executive of Dairen, the Consul-General at Mukden, besides the President of the South Manchuria Railway itself. These four officers must meet and exchange views at Dairen before anything is undertaken. What is discussed in the meeting held in camera often leaks out to the Chinese authorities of the Three Eastern Provinces. They in turn would try to obstruct any forward movements of the South Manchuria Railway authorization; it again has to run the gauntlet at the Departments of Foreign Affairs, of Railways, of Finance and of Army. If these ministers do not agree, the matter is dropped. Therefore, although the present prime minister realises his own incompetence, he has nevertheless taken concurrently the portfolio of foreign affairs, so that our movements in Manchuria may be kept confidential and the execution of our plans may be swift and decisive. On account of these reasons, the South Manchuria Railway should be radically reorganized. [The reorganization of the South Manchuria Railway as proposed in the Tanaka Memorial, actually took place as outlined on October 1, 1936, coincident with the thirtieth anniversary of the administration of the Kwantung Leased Territory and the Port of Dairen. This reorganization was about as indicated in the Tanaka Memorial, involving two significant steps: (1) introduction of a unified management of all railways in Manchuria and North Korea and (2) creation of a subsidiary Industry Department which emphasized the necessity for the general economic development of Manchuria.] All appurtenant enterprises which are profit-making should be made independent companies under the wings of the South Manchuria Railroad so that we may take determined steps on the conquest of Manchuria and Mongolia. On the other hand, Chinese, Europeans and Americans should be invited to invest money in the South Manchuria Railway on the condition that we have a plurality of its stocks. In that event the control of the company is in our hands, and our mission from the empire can be discharged more vigorously. In short, by inviting international participation in the South Manchuria Railway, we can blind the eyes of the world. Having achieved that, we can push our advance in Manchuria and Mongolia at our will, free ourselves from the restraints of the Nine Power Treaty and strengthen our activities in that country with foreign capital. The important appurtenant enterprises of the South Manchuria Railway are: Iron and Steel. Iron and steel are closely connected with national development. Every country to-day attaches great importance to it. But because of the lack of ores, we have found no solution to this problem. Hitherto we have had to import steel from the Yangtse Valley and the Malay Peninsula. But according to a secret survey of our General Staff, a wealth of iron mines are found in many places in Manchuria and Mongolia. A conservative estimate of the reserve is 10 billion tons. At first when there was a lack of technique, the Anshan Iron and Steel Works was involved in an annual loss of Yen 3,000,000. Later, new methods were discovered, and the technique developed so that during 1926 the loss was only Yen 150,000 and a year later there was a profit of Yen 800,000. If the furnace is improved, we ought to earn at least Yen 4,000,000 a year. The quality of the ore at Penhsihu is excellent. However Japan has insistently invited the United States to invest money in the development of Manchuria. Even after the outbreak of the undeclared war in China, Japanese financiers and diplomatic officials launched an ambitious campaign of publicity in the United States with the object of securing a loan of $50,000,000 (for the development of heavy industries in Manchuria.) Placing it with the Anshan Iron Works, we shall have the comfort of being self-sufficient in iron and steel. The iron deposits in Manchuria and Mongolia are estimated at 1,200,000,000 tons, and the coal deposits 2,500,000,000 tons. This coal ought to be sufficient for smelting the iron ores. With such large amounts of iron and coal at our disposal, we ought to be self-sufficient for at least seventy years. At the rate of $100.00 profit on each ton of steel, for 350,000,000 tons of steel we shall have a profit of Yen 35,000,000,000. This is a tremendous asset to our economic resources. We shall save the expense of Yen 120,000,000 which we pay for the importation of steel every year. When we can have sufficient iron and steel for our own industries, we shall have acquired the secret for becoming the leading nation in the world. Thus strengthened, we can conquer both the East and the West. In order to attain this goal, the iron works must be separated from the South Manchuria Railway. Such unified control will keep China from preventing us to become self-sufficient in iron and steel. Petroleum. Another important commodity which we lack is petroleum. It is also essential to the existence of a nation. Fortunately, there lie in the Fushun Coal Mine 5,200,000,000 tons of shale oil, from every hundred catties of which six catties of crude oil may be extracted. By means of American machinery, every hundred catties will yield nine catties of refined oil good for motor cars and battleships. At present Japan imports from foreign countries 700,000 tons of mineral oils every year valued at Yen 60,000,000. These figures are on the increase. As there are 50 billion tons of shale in the Fushun mines, the yield calculated at 5 per cent would be 250,000,000 tons; at 9 per cent, 450,000,000 tons of oil. Taking an average of the two, the yield would be 350,000,000 tons, and assuming the value of the oil to be fifteen yen a ton, the oil shale contained in the Fushun Mine would bring us Yen 2,250,000,000. This will be a great industrial revolution for us. From the standpoint of national defense and national wealth, petroleum is a great factor. Having the iron and petroleum of Manchuria, our army and navy will become impregnable walls of defense. That Manchuria and Mongolia are the heart and liver of our empire, is a truthful saying. For the sake of our empire, we should be congratulated.

Agricultural Fertilizer – Ammonia Sulphate and Other Products

Agricultural fertilizer is a great necessity for the production of foodstuffs. Chemical fertilizers depend upon the ammonia sulphate extracted from coal. The Fushun coal yields especially good results. At present, our total consumption of ammonia sulphate is 500,000 tons. Of this, only half is manufactured at home, using the coal from the Kailan or the Fushun Mining Companies. The remaining half is imported from abroad at the cost of Yen 35,000,000 a year. With our agricultural work daily increasing and in view of the development of our new empire in Manchuria and Mongolia, we shall easily need 1,000,000 tons of ammonia sulphate every year during the next ten years. From the soot gathered from the burning of Fushun coal connected with the manufacture of steel, we could produce large quantities of ammonia sulphate. If the yield is put at 300,000 tons a year, we shall add an annual income of more than Yen 40,000,000. In fifty years, this will mount up to Yen 2,000,000,000. This money could be used for the improvement of our agriculture. If there is any surplus, we can buy bean cakes with it and then invade the farms all over China and in the South Sea Islands. In order to accomplish this, we must separate this enterprise from the South Manchuria Railway. We shall then be able to control the fertilizers of the Far East. Soda and Soda Ash We import 100,000 tons of Soda Ash at the cost of more than Yen 10,000,000 a year. Both soda and soda ash are valuable materials for military and industrial purposes. Soda is derived from nothing more than salt and coal, both of which are cheap and abundant in Manchuria and Mongolia. If we go into this manufacture, we can supply not only ourselves but can also sell it to China with a view to controlling its industrial products. We ought to gain from it a profit of at least Yen 150,000,000 a year. We can also supply our own military and chemical needs. Again this industry must be separated from the South Manchuria Railway.

Magnesium and Aluminum
According to the independent surveys of the South Manchuria Railway Company and Dr. Honta of Tohoku University, magnesite and aluminium is a very promising business (in Manchuria). Magnesium is found in the surroundings of Tashichiao, and aluminium in the vicinity of Yentai. The deposit is one of the largest in the world. A ton of magnesite is worth Yen 2,000 and a ton of aluminium is worth about Yen 1,700. An estimate of the deposits of both

minerals in Manchuria is Yen 750,000,000. These substances are especially useful for making aeroplanes, mess kits in the army, hospital apparatus and vessels, and other important industries. The United States alone has extensive deposits of these substances. The output of our country is one ton a year! Such materials are becoming more useful every day, but the supply is insufficient. Its price is growing high, as if never reaching a limit. The deposits in our territory of Manchuria and Mongolia are nothing less than a God-given gift. This metal is really precious, being indispensable to both our industry and national defense. It also should be made an independent business, separate from the South Manchuria Railway. Its manufacture should be in Japan, so as to keep the Fengtien Government from imitating it on the one hand and to avoid the watchful eyes of the British and American capitalists on the other. After we have gained control of it in the Three Eastern Provinces, we may harness the water power of the Yalu River to work on these metal ores. In view of the development of aircraft, in the future all the world will come to us for the materials necessary for aeronautics. If all the enterprises mentioned above were made in dependent undertakings, they would make rapid progress and bring us at least a profit of 60 billion yen a year. The industrial development in South Manchuria means much to our national defense and economic progress. It will help us to build the foundation of an industrial empire. As to the cultural undertakings such as hospitals, schools and philanthropic institutions, they are our signal towers in our advance into Manchuria and Mongolia. They are the institutions for spreading our national prestige and power. More specifically they are the baits for rights and privileges. Let us separate all these from the South Manchuria Railway in order that we may redouble our efforts and advance into

North Manchuria to reclaim the sources of great wealth there. When these important undertakings become independent and are free to develop without the interference of our officials, they will naturally become channels of national prosperity. On the wings of economic development, we could make rapid advance without either arousing the suspicion of the Powers or the anti-Japanese activities of the people of the Three Eastern Provinces. Such hidden methods would enable us to build the New Continental Empire with ease and efficiency. The foreign loans for the South Manchuria Railway must be confined to those railroads already completed. Other railways built by us but nominally under Chinese control, can either be amalgamated with the completed lines or made independent according to the desire of the investing nations. The slogan of 'Equal Opportunity' helps us to get foreign loans as well as to dispel suspicion of our designs in North Manchuria. At any rate, we shall need foreign capital to develop our Continental Empire. When the South Manchuria Railway is open to foreign investments the Powers will be glad to lend more to us and China can do nothing to block it. This is an excellent way to further our plans in Manchuria. We should lose no time in doing it. As to the wealth concentrated in the northern part of Manchuria and Mongolia, we should do likewise. The two new railways from Kirin to Hueining and from Changchun to Talai, as well as the lumber and mining interests, should also be managed as separate institutions. The South Manchuria Railway will also be greatly enriched by our exploits in North Manchuria. In undertaking this, we must permit foreign investment on the South Manchuria Railway so that any profit that it makes is shared by other nations. When they share in the profits, no one will interfere with our activities in North Manchuria. Already Chinese immigrants are pouring into South Manchuria in large numbers. Their position will become stronger every day. As the right of renting land in the interior is not yet secured, our immigrants are gradually losing ground. Even if our government's backing will maintain our people there, they cannot compete with the Chinese due to the latter's low standard of living. Our only chance now is to defeat the Chinese by heavy capitalization. This again necessitates the use of foreign loans. This is so, especially because the riches of North Manchuria are even not accessible to the Chinese immigrants. We must seize the present opportunity, and hasten the progress of immigration by our own people and take possession of all rights there so as to shut out the Chinese. But in order to encourage immigration, rapid transportation is essential. This will afford both facilities to our people and bring the natural resources there to the would-be market. Moreover, both Russia and ourselves have been increasing armaments. On account of geographical positions, we have conflicting interests. If we want to obtain the wealth of North Manchuria and to build up the New Continent according to the will of Emperor Meiji, we must rush our people into North Manchuria first and seek to break the friendship between Russia and China. In this way, we can enjoy the wealth of North Manchuria and hold at bay both Russia and China. In case of war, our immigrants in North Manchuria will combine with our forces in South Manchuria and at one stroke settle the problem forever. In case this is not possible, they can still maintain their own in North Manchuria and supply the rest of us with foodstuffs and raw materials. As the interests of North Manchuria and our country are so wrapped up, we could march directly into North Manchuria and pursue our settled policy. The Necessity of Establishing a Colonial Department. Our exploitation of Manchuria takes a variety of forms. Often those in authority take such different views that even the most profitable undertaking for our country cannot be carried out. Because of the lack of speed, our secrets are often exposed and are made propaganda materials by the Mukden Government much to the detriment of our country in international relations. Whenever a new undertaking is projected in Manchuria and Mongolia, it will become the subject of discussion of tens of meetings and conferences in Dairen. Not only the approval of the four-headed government there is necessary, but also the sanction of the cabinet at home has to be secured before anything can be carried out. Because of all these obstacles, any undertaking will take months and months before any definite results are seen. In the process it is possible for the Chinese to employ Japanese adventurers to steal our secrets so that before a project is launched it is often reported to the Chinese and in turn it becomes common property of the world. We are suddenly brought under the check of world opinion, and more than once we have incurred hardship in putting into practice our policy toward Manchuria and Mongolia. Furthermore, the opposition party has also made capital out of what they find in these regions in order to attack the government. All these have many serious results with our diplomatic relations. Henceforth, we must change our practice in order to proceed more adroitly. The centre of control must be in Tokyo. That will (1) insure secrecy; (2) stop China from knowing beforehand our plans; (3) avoid the suspicion of the powers before the thing is done; (4) unify the multiple control in Manchuria and (5) bring the government agencies in Manchuria and Mongolia in close touch with the central government so as to deal with China with undivided power. For these reasons we should follow the original plan for absorbing Korea laid down by Ito and Katsura and establish a Colonial Department, the special function of which is to look after the expansion in Manchuria and Mongolia. The administration of Formosa, Korea and Saghalien Island may be its nominal function, but our expansion in Manchuria and Mongolia is its real purpose. This will blind the eyes of the world on the one hand and forestall the disclosure of secrets on the other. It is my personal conviction that the fact that the absorption of Korea could not be effected during the administration of Ito, was due to the lack of a special office for Control. Therefore, there were always differences of opinion and secret policies were impossible. Such a state of affairs played into the hands of international obstruction and Korean opposition. Then a number of propagandists went to Europe and America as well as Korea itself, declaring that we firmly respected the independence of Korea and had no designs on an inch of Korean territory. The result of their work was the recovery of international confidence. After that, a Colonial Department was established under the pretence of being intended for Formosa. Then we seized the opportunity and the object was gained! It goes to prove that in order to undertake colonization and immigration, a special office for it is absolutely necessary. Moreover, the creation of a new empire in Mongolia and Manchuria is of utmost importance to the existence of Japan. It is necessary to have a special office, in order that the politics in that vast territory may be from Tokyo. The officers in the field should not only take orders, they should not interfere with the execution of policies where they please. This will insure secrecy; and the opposition nations have no chance of getting into the secrets of our colonial activities. Then our movements regarding Mongolia and Manchuria will be beyond the reach of international public opinion and we shall be free from interferences. As to the subsidiary enterprises of the South Manchuria Railway such as the Development Company, the Land Company, and the Trust Company, the power of supervision and planning should also be in the colonial office. They should all be under united control in order that they may all help in the general policy of expansion in Mongolia and Manchuria of the Imperial Government and complete the creation of the new empire.

The Taling River Valley on the Peking-Mukden Railway
The Taling River Valley is a wide area sparsely populated but infested with bandits. Many Koreans have made investments here, especially in rice fields. Judging from its resources, this region is bound to be prosperous. It will also be an advantageous foothold for us if we want to expand into the Jehol region. We should give full protection to our Korean subjects here and wait for an opportunity to secure from China the right of colonization so that our immigrants may live here and act as our vanguards to Jehol and Mongolia. In case of warfare, this valley will be a strategic point to quarter large armies of soldiers. We shall then not only check the Chinese soldiers from advancing north, but also hold the key to the immense wealth of South Manchuria. When Koreans come into this region we should finance them through our Trust and other financial organs with a view to gaining for these organs the actual ownership while the Koreans may satisfy themselves with the right of farming only. Ostensibly the ownership of land must reside with the Koreans. It is a convenient way of securing rights from the Chinese government. Henceforth the Trust companies and financial organs should give them full backing when our own and Korean subjects wish to gain land ownership. If they need money to buy farms from the Chinese, the financial organs should also come to their aid. Unnoticeably we shall gain

control of the better rice fields which we may give to our own immigrants. They shall displace the Koreans who in turn may go on opening new fields, to deliver to the convenient use of our own people. This is the policy with respect to the colonization of rice fields and bean farms. As to the policy for herd farming, the Development Company should be especially entrusted gradually to expand, eventually placing all the wealth of herds at the disposal of our country. This same company may also take care of horse breeding and select the best out of Mongolia for the use of our national defense.

Precaution against Chinese Migration
Recently the internal disturbances in China have driven large hordes of immigrants into Mongolia and Manchuria, thereby threatening the advance of our migration. For the sake of our activities in this field, we should not fail to take precautions. The fact that the Chinese government welcomes this migration and does nothing to hold back the tide oppresses our policy even more seriously. A noted American has made the statement the Mukden authorities are carrying out such effective government that all people are moving into their territory. Therefore, the influx of immigrants is looked upon as a mark of effective government of Mukden authorities. We, of course, are concerned. Unless we put a stop to it, in less than ten years our own policy of emigration will prove an instrument for China to crush us with. Politically we must use police force to check this tendency as much as possible and economically our financiers should drive the Chinese out with low wages. Furthermore, we must develop and expand electric power to displace human labor. This will keep out Chinese immigrants as well as monopolise the control of motor force as a first step toward controlling the industries

development of this vast region. Hospitals and Schools Hospitals and schools in Manchuria must be independent of the South Manchuria Railway, for the people have often considered these institutions of imperialism and refuse to have anything to do with them. When these are separated and made independent institutions we shall be able to make the people realize our goodness so that they will be thankful to us ... But in establishing schools emphasis should be laid on normal schools for men and women. Through these in educational work we may build up a substantial goodwill among the people toward Japan. This is our first principle of cultural structure.[3]

It is important that the whole Tanaka Memorial document was presented here for the historian to read and understand. Given the fact that Young China Publishing managed to get a copy of this document in 1936, it is amazing that any historian would consider it a plant, for no one was smart enough in Russia or China to write up such a precise document as this showing exactly what Japan would do in the future, and Japan followed this document to a tee.

As Carl Crow wrote about the Tanaka memorial:

Japanese have officially denied the existence of the Tanaka memorial though its existence is hinted at in a magazine article by Fuanosuka Kuhura, who was Minister of Communications at the time of the conference in Manchuria. There is no doubt that the conference was held in Manchuria at the time stated and that its purpose was to draw up a program of policy for Japan to follow in China and Manchuria and Mongolia. It would have been a most extraordinary thing for a conference of that sort to be held without embodying the results in a report, and he was Premier of the country, it was the duty of Baron Tanaka to present this report to the Emperor. The fact that a huge number of Japanese officials participated in this conference, that many of these Japanese had Chinese servants made the task of espionage easy, so that this document could have fell into Chinese hands very easy. But the credibility of the report need not rest on any of these circumstances, nor be weakened by Japanese Official denials. It does not contain a word which does not fit in with the well-known ideas of policies of Baron Tanaka and the group of militarists of whom he was the leader. If the memorial was never written and never presented to the Emperor, then it is a huge coincidence and is very curious and unaccountable circumstance that it should form the basis for Japanese policy throughout the war.[4]

It was Japan's plan that if the Axis had won the Second World War, it would have achieved the next to last final part of Baron Tanaka's programme. With Japan in control of the vast resources in material and manpower in East Asia she would only have to wait and organise until the appropriate moment to invade Europe and conquer, then place all the white races of the world under control of Imperial Japan. There is no doubt that this document found a way to come into FDR's hands way before the attack on Pearl Harbor, and yet he did nothing to increase the defence of America or even strengthen its defences. Actually when he first took office, one of the first things he did was to cut defence spending. If anything he could have easily created jobs by putting people to work making defence arms, yet he did not. Japan was gearing up for a war with the United States and from all indications our leaders were asleep.

As Itabashi Koshu wrote: 'That is why it served to inflame passions for everyone; for Japan it was a scared war. Japan claimed it would unite the 8 corners of the world under one roof; not that it was fighting for territory gain.'[5] Itabashi was 10 years old when he heard this in 1936. This is exactly what the Tanaka Memorial said.

Chapter III

Pearl Harbor Naval War Games, 1932

The evidence from the naval war games in 1932 is the one thing that should have jumped out and smacked our political leaders in the face for it showed just how weak our defences were at Pearl Harbor. Below should be the after-actions report of this exercise, but it is still classified under national security regulations. Instead you can read this. Also, remember the after-action report was changed to fit the Navy agenda as the original by Admiral Yarnell was dismissed showing the failure of the Pearl Harbor defences.

It was a quiet Sunday morning. The winter storms that routinely lashed the sea north-east of Oahu were at it again, pouring rain on Kahuka Point and obscuring most of the horizon with low clouds, though right over Pearl Harbor, the sky was clear. The fleet lay at anchor, in the neat double rows on battleship row, at the small submarine base, and even in the dry docks, having their hulls scraped and checked for the corrosion that the saltwater carved into their sides.

The sun had only just risen. A minimum of crew was on call. Some were sleeping off the effects of the night before. Others were at their homes on shore, with their families, undoubtedly looking forward to a relaxing day at church and playing with their children. A few were already stumbling into kitchens and restaurants and mess halls, seeking that morning cup of coffee and a bite of breakfast.

Suddenly, aeroplanes shot out of the clouds, strafing the ground, dropping bombs on the peaceful ships at harbour. In moments, the harbour was in disarray, men scrambling to gain their battle stations, but it was already too late. The ships were already damaged, some severely, both at anchor and those in the dry docks. Nothing was spared.

The planes headed back out to sea, and there, in the midst of the storm, a small group of ships waited for their return, hiding in the rain, safe from the eyes of radar. The planes landed safely on the two carriers.

In the bridge of the lead carrier, the admiral listened with satisfaction to reports of the damage. When presented with the final report, he smiled, and signed it: Adm. Harry E. Yarnell, USS Saratoga, Sunday, February 7, 1932.

That's right. Pearl Harbor was first attacked on 7 February 1932, nine years before the date that will live in infamy. On 7 December, the United States pauses to remember the attack of the Japanese on Pearl Harbor, and the lives lost there, but few know that the attack had been eerily foretold nine years earlier.

See, in the beginning of the twentieth century, the backbone of the Navy was the behemoth battleships and destroyers. Aircraft carriers and submarines were considered little more than niche vessels that had limited uses.

But one admiral, Harry Yarnell, believed that the Navy had more to fear from an aerial attack delivered from the deck of a carrier than from ever larger confrontations between larger and larger ships and deck guns. During the annual combined Navy war games at Pearl Harbor, he set out to prove his point. Every year, Yarnell's ships in California would leave for Pearl, 'attacking' the battleships stationed in Pearl. (At this time the military's main Pacific base was in San Diego, not Pearl Harbor, so Yarnell had the larger fleet.) Usually, the radio traffic between the massive fleet would be intercepted by Pearl, their battleships would leave harbour, and they would 'battle' out in the open sea.

In 1932, however, Yarnell left most of his allotted ships in California with orders to maintain radio silence. He took the aircraft carriers *Saratoga* and *Lexington* out to sea with a small escort of three destroyers. They travelled under radio silence, staying away from the travelled freighter lanes, and sought an area where they could not be seen from the radar towers on Hawaii. During the winter months, storms routinely occurred near Oahu, and here he hid, knowing the radar could not see them, and no freighter would be near. To top it all off, he also decided to attack on Sunday, a day he knew was the day most sailors would be off duty, and also most likely to be off ship.

The 'bombs' and 'strafing' were just flares and bags of flour, but the referees of the war games judged that Yarnell had been more than successful, sinking *every* ship in Pearl Harbor, as well as figuratively destroying every land-based plane in Oahu. In addition, twenty-four hours after the raid, using what few battleships that had been at sea during the simulated attack, the Pearl Harbor team had not been able to locate Yarnell's small fleet. From Yarnell's point of view, it had been a complete success, and he and his officers argued that, having proved the effectiveness of an aerial attack from a carrier, they should become more central to the plans of the military, instead of outlying support vehicles for the battleships.

But it was also an idea ahead of its time. The admirals, who believed that the battleship was still the workhorse of the navy, protested the results, insisting that if this was a real scenario, their battleships would have found the aircraft carriers and destroyed them first.

In the end, the battleship officers won, and in the years between 1932 and 1941, the military and FDR ordered the construction of another twelve battleships but only four aircraft carriers, the *Yorktown*, *Enterprise*, *Wasp* and *Hornet* (and only *Enterprise* was supposed to be assigned to the Pacific Fleet, where Yarnell feared a Japanese attack.) The Navy was growing, but the retired Yarnell feared that it was growing the wrong sectors.

What few knew, was the Japanese paid attention to this particular war game, and sent a detailed record to Tokyo about how the surprise was accomplished. Records later showed that the Japanese War College studied this attack in 1936, coming to the following conclusion: 'In case the enemy's main fleet is berthed at Pearl Harbor, the idea should be to open hostilities by surprise attack from the air.'

The stage was set, and the Japanese, believing that they would not be able to withstand the full might of the American Navy if the United

States entered the Pacific conflict, decided to take out the fleet at Pearl Harbor, following the pattern set in 1932 by Rear Admiral Yarnell. Their fleet travelled in radio silence, they travelled off the well-travelled shipping lanes of the Pacific, they hid in the foul winter weather, and attacked just after dawn on a Sunday.

'The bombs weren't flour bags, on this, the third attack of Pearl Harbor, and 2,896 men and women died; military as well as civilians.'[1] Here is a prime example of information that was in FDR's hands and he did nothing to fix. It was even covered up.

> "The fact that some documents relating to the attack are still classified has also provided much intelligent information to the conspiracy theorists. There is signal intelligence obtained by the British 'Ultra' and the U.S. 'Magic' programs relating to Pearl Harbor, for example, which is still secret. In addition, there are also reports of other documents, for example, a purported, explicit warning from military intelligence in the Dutch East Indies of an impending Japanese attack on Pearl Harbor, that are still classified. There is also the fact that many documents at Pearl Harbor were destroyed in the weeks following the attack for fear of an impending Japanese invasion.
>
> One historical fact that is not open to dispute, however, is the mock raid on Pearl Harbor on 7 February 1932. In the period between the Washington Naval Conference in 1921 and 1940, the U.S. did not have a two-ocean navy. The main Pacific anchorages were in San Diego and San Francisco, where the fleet could be deployed quickly in the defence of the Panama Canal or of the Hawaiian Islands. Its proximity to the canal also allowed for its rapid transfer to the Atlantic should it be needed there.
>
> 'Planners' at the War Department had been considering the possibility of war with Japan since at least 1906. The eventual strategy, dubbed War Plan Orange, anticipated that in the Pearl

vent of a war with Japan, the Philippines and American bases in the western Pacific would be either blockaded or overrun. In the interim, the U.S. Pacific Fleet would concentrate its strength along the West Coast until the ships had received their full complement of crew. During the 1930s, ships operated with only half of their allotted crew as an economy measure. Once the fleet had been readied, it would sail west to relieve the Philippines. With the Philippines secured, the fleet would proceed to blockade Japan and seek a decisive naval showdown with the Japanese fleet."[2]

"During Fleet Problem XIII and Grand Joint Exercise 4 Vice Admiral Harry Yarnell showed the rest of the Navy what the aircraft carrier could do. In the war game between two naval forces (blue vs. black) Yarnell (commanding blue) chose a different approach in confronting the black team. Rather than have the battleships fight it out in horizon-to-horizon shelling, he brought his force of two aircraft carriers (the *Lexington* and the *Saratoga*) and four destroyers (all under radio silence) from California to the home base of the black team at Pearl. Operating beyond the normal shipping lanes and squalls he was able to successfully approach the base without being detected and launched 157 planes against the ships and the defending aircraft (which was still on the ground). Committing imaginary strafing Yarnell's attacking force decimated the defending aircraft; and in dropping flour-sack bombs the attacking force pulverized the ships docked at Pearl. It was an extraordinary victory for the blue team, and it should have been a monumental wake-up for all those decision makers involved in running the Navy.

In spite of the obvious victory by Yarnell, the exercise was seen as something as a fluke, and the umpires evaluating the judged the use of the aircraft carrier in a possible attack on Pearl Harbor to be 'doubtful'.

> In his review of the exercise Yarnell clearly stated that the aircraft carrier should become the main arm of the U.S. Navy – it would certainly be so for other navies, including potential enemy navies, thereby putting the U.S. on an unequal footing should this course of action not be followed. He was certain that he demonstrated that a major change was due in American naval tactics and strategy, and that in order to fight a transoceanic war that six to eight aircraft carriers would be necessary."[3]

This is absolutely ludicrous for the planes would have been destroyed before they ever left the ground. In any event, the battleship commanders didn't want to see time and effort and money removed from their own projects, and so the Yarnell results were dismissed.

This is exactly why in 1941 the attack came off so well for the Japanese, for over 90 per cent of U.S. aircraft on the ground were destroyed.

What any historian should be asking here is why is this information still being classified top secret by our government? The fact that the reports on Fleet Problem XIII and Grand Joint Exercise 4 cannot be viewed at the American National Archives or the Library of Congress should send a red flag to any historian or scholar. The other thing that should truly concern any historian is that this information was right there for FDR to view and make his own conclusions about. This is the exact type of information that should have warned FDR that U.S. defences at Pearl Harbor were inadequate and in need of major improvements to prepare them to defend an attack. The question to ask oneself is why did not FDR do this once he became the commander in chief for he definitely had the power to do so?

The thing that the historian needs to remember here is that these are facts, not conspiracy theories but documents that have been written up showing America's vulnerability in the Pacific along with the possibility of going to war with Imperial Japan during this time. The excuse that America was looking for isolationism from Europe is one thing, but this was not the case in the Pacific where the U.S. had an army in the Philippines and an Army and Navy base in the Hawaiian Islands. There was no isolationism there. U.S. intelligence was telling it that Japan was gearing up for a war with China, possibly every Asian country in the Pacific (which did come to pass), and if FDR had even took a quick look at *Winged Defense*, The Tanaka Memorial, and the Fleet Problem XIII and Grand Joint Exercise 4 he should have realised the probability of a war with the Imperial Japanese when he took office in January 1933. If he did not realise this, then this should surely rate him as the least effective President the United States has ever had.

What should make any true blue American angry is that FDR with this and other information that you will read in the coming chapters set up the country's sailors, soldiers, and marines to die at Pearl Harbor and the Philippines when they did not have to. The Bataan Death March in the Philippines was the worst atrocity committed by the Japanese, but even after the attack on Pearl Harbor and the Philippines, the U.S. still had a good chance of getting those young men out in late December 1941. However, FDR left those brave young men there to die or become PoWs. The ages of these young enlisted men was from 17 to 19 on average, with some as young as 16.

The question a historian should ask here is how did FDR allow this to happen? The answer is simple: he did not care. As will be revealed in later chapters, FDR could have prevented the attack on Pearl Harbor on 7 December 1941 and the invasion of the Philippines in December 1941, for he had the information in front of him to see to the protection of these soldiers, sailors and marines. The soldiers in the Philippines had outdated First World War weapons, and then they did not even have enough of those. Many troops did not even have a rifle. However, instead of sending military supplies and arms to the Philippines, he instead choose to send arms to the Soviet Union (who did not need them) and Britain, making U.S. young soldiers sitting ducks for an attack by the Imperial Japanese Army. These young soldiers could have been saved if they had the weapons sent to Russia and the rest of Europe.

The truth about Pearl Harbor that any historian should understand is that it was left wide open for an attack by the Imperial Japanese Navy. The evidence is right there in front of anyone who is willing to put in the time and effort to do the proper research to find these documents to prove that FDR knew when and where the Japanese were going to attack the American forces in the Pacific. To not report the truth is a crime perpetrated on the relatives of these men who died there and it is also a crime committed on history, for the truth should be told even if the heavens should fall.

Chapter IV

Japanese Naval Academy Pearl Harbor Question of 1935/Unit 731

The information that was available to President Franklin D. Roosevelt was in abundance even before 1937 and the sinking of the gunboat USS *Panay* and the Nanking Massacre. To begin with there is the problem of the final exam question to Japanese naval cadets who graduated from the Japanese Naval Academy in 1935 right up to the attack on Pearl Harbor. What was that question that scholars and historians should know but most do not, 'How would you conduct a surprise attack on Pearl Harbor?' There is no doubt that intelligence spies the U.S. had working in Japan at this time found out about this question and sent this information back to FDR. Again here is important information confirming that the President did not take any precautions at Pearl Harbor. The truly amazing thing is the ignorance of historians on this event, for if you search the web you will find nothing on this highly significant information. The only place that I found a small reference to it was in the National Archives and the Library of Congress. None of the EDU sites contain any thesis PDFs on this subject matter. So we see that the U.S. advanced college education system is failing to teach true history and instead the lies of a politically correct history. Any history of the Pearl Harbor attack should have this vital information included.

Now for a history that was quite well hidden by both the Japanese and United States governments up until the 1980s; the experiments of Japanese Unit 731. Unit 731 was begun in 1931 and its commander was Major General Shiro Ishii. This was a top secret Imperial Japanese Army biological weapons programme. It performed inhumane experiments on Chinese civilians and Russian and American PoWs.

The thing that is amazing here is that we have allowed these Japanese war criminals to go free but we still to this day hunt down Nazi war criminals. In 2015 there was a Nazi clerk/bus driver who stood trial at 95 and was found guilty. However, thousands of Japanese war criminals lived or are still living free and were never brought to justice. Some of the worst criminals, including Hisato Yoshimura, who was in charge of the frostbite experiments, went on to occupy key medical and other posts in the public and private sectors.

As you can see from these photos, it is obvious that what was going on here were crimes against humanity. These photos would also find their way into FDR's hands way before the attack on Pearl Harbor or the attack on USS *Panay* in 1937. And what did FDR do about these atrocities? Absolutely nothing. Here was a perfect time to have declared war on Japan, with these photos, the photos of the Nanking Massacre and the attack on the *Panay* in 1937 he had more than ample reason to go to war with Imperial Japan.

If FDR knew about these atrocities that were being committed and did nothing about them then much like Elie Wiesel wrote in *After the Darkness: Reflections of the Holocaust* (New York, Schocken Books, 2002), FDR was as much to blame as Hitler for the death of the Jews in the camps. Wiesel has received many different honours, including the Presidential Medal of Freedom, the United States Congressional Gold Medal, the French Legion of Honor/Rank of the Grand Cross and the 1986 Nobel Peace Prize and is considered an expert on Nazi concentration camps. FDR and Churchill were both told that if they would give these Jews visas in 1938 that Germany would release them to go to their countries. However, they would not give them visas. How many lives could they have saved?

To a certain extent America and England should have to share the blame for some of the Holocaust. The United States and England are much to blame here for they would not open their immigration ports to accept these Jews from Germany. It was up to the country they were going to determine if they should be given a visa or not to be admitted. However, those who wanted to emigrate could do so without too many bureaucratic delays, as long as they had a visa from a country that would take them. Great scientific, culture, and economic leaders were able to leave Stefan Zweig, Kurt Weill, and Sigmund Warburg were among those lucky enough to make it to London, Paris, Amsterdam or New York. A visa would free a prisoner in Dachau or Buchenwald. But for the average citizen, emigration was harder; the free world did not want them. The International Conference in Evian, France, in 1938 made that clear. The conference, organized purportedly to help German and Austrian refugees, instead provided rich entertainment for readers of Nazi newspapers. The eloquent participants explained the reasons why their governments couldn't host potential emigrants. Joseph Goebbels, Hitler's chief propagandist, chuckled in public, as if to say: Look at all these hypocritical countries berating us for not wanting to live with Jews! They are supposedly so generous and charitable, but how are they different from us? On this shameful point he was absolutely right. Franklin D. Roosevelt and Winston Churchill are as much to blame for not accepting these Jewish refugees into their countries the United States and England, as Hitler is for ordering there extermination in the Nazi concentration camps.[1] How many would have survived if only the United States and England had opened their doors for them to come in. The fact that these Jews could not leave Germany caused an even deeper hatred by Adolph Hitler that he would order the mass termination of all the Jews in Germany. This war crime would become known as "The Final Solution."

Roosevelt's bigotry showed through at the Yalta conference Roosevelt was still telling jokes about Jews, when FDR mentioned to Stalin that he would be seeing Saudi Arabian leader Ibn Saud, Stalin asked if he intended to make any concessions to the king, President Roosevelt replied according to the transcript, that "there is only one concession he thought he might offer and that was to give him the six million Jews in the United States."[2] (Of course this would have led to another mass slaughter and FDR knew it. So of course it was a joke to FDR that should have never been said to Stalin.)

If FDR, with the knowledge he had on the atrocities that were committed in Nanking, gone to war with Japan in 1938 after the attack on the *Panay* on the Yangtze River he could have prevented the attack on Pearl Harbor and the Bataan Death March in the Philippines, saving countless lives.

Below are two documents from the Unit 731 file, which was kept from the American public until the late 1980s.

```
                                    Satoyamabe-mura, Higashi Tsukuma-gun,
                                    Nagano Prefecture
                                                           Aug. 23 1946

CI&E, GHQ, SCAP

Report on War Criminals.

         Motoji Yamaguchi, a former veterinary surgeon major
              Address:    Murata-cho, Shibata-gun, Miyagi Prefecture
         Yujiro Wakamatsu, a former veterinary surgeon major-general
              Address:    Hagi-shi, Otsu-gun, Yamaguchi Prefecture
         Hozaka, a former veterinary surgeon lieutenant-colonel
              Address     Unknown

    The above veterinary surgeons dissected many war prisoners of the
Allied Forces at the outdoor dissecting ground of No. 100 Army Corps at
Hsinking (Changchun), Manchuria, as their inspections of the cattle plague.
If you would investigate these criminals, you will find many other persons
who have participated to the dissections. There are a number of the witness
of the inspections.

                                                   Yours truly
                                                   Takeshi Nishimura
```

DECLASSIFIED
Nazi War Crimes Disclosure Act
PL105-246
By: [signature] Date: [signature]

Date: 6 December 1946

Report of Investigation Division, Legal Section, GHQ, SCAP.

Inv. Div. No. 1117	CRD No.	Report by: Neal R. Smith 1st Lt., Inf.

Title: Infectious Disease Research Laboratory.
(DENSEMBYO KENKYSHO)

Synopsis of facts:

Letter written to General MacArthur by Hisashi OKADA reflects that bacteriological experiments were conducted on POWs at the Infectious Disease Research Laboratory, Tokyo. Names of doctors responsible, given by writer.

- F -

DETAILS:

At Tokyo:

This report was predicated upon the receipt of a letter written to General MacArthur by Hisashi OKADA, Tokyo-to, Suginami-ku, Izumi-cho, 62.

A check of Investigation Division files revealed no information regarding OKADA, writer of said letter.

Criminal Registry Division indices show that OKADA is not on the requested apprehended lists.

The following is a digest of letter received after being translated by ATIS, the original of which is being transmitted with CRD copy of this report and entered as Exhibit "1". Translation of letter is submitted with report as Exhibit "2".

"The writer requests a full investigation of the persons who conducted bacteriological experimentations on PsW which resulted in three deaths. The late OKAMOTO, Akira (   ), assistant professor at Infectious Diseases Research Laboratory (DENSEMBYO KENKYUSHO) of TOKYO-To, SHIBA-Ku assumed the responsibility for the experiments and committed suicide last year. The writer and friends of OKAMOTO know that another person was the originator of the experimentations and was actually responsible for the deaths.

Chapter V

The Attack on USS *Panay*, 1937

If there was ever a reason to go to war with Japan before the attack on Pearl Harbor it would have to be the attack by Japanese planes on the United States Gunship *Panay* on the Yangtze River in China in 1937.

This was more than enough for America to declare war on Japan. Even before the attack on the *Panay*, Secretary of State Cordell Hull feared that with an attack on Nanking, Americans could be in danger from Japanese pilots. Douglas Peifer wrote:

> Hull's misgivings were justified. As Japan proceeded with military operations around Shanghai and then pushed up the Yangtze River toward the Republic of China's capital at Nanking, a growing number of complaints reached the US Embassy about incidents in which Americans had been hurt, attacked, or witnessed brutal attacks on Chinese employees and civilian facilities. On the 17th of September, Ambassador Joseph Grew lodged an official complaint with the Japanese government, noting that Japanese military forces were showing a reckless disregard for US lives and property. Japanese aircraft, Grew admonished, had even subjected American humanitarian and philanthropic establishments in China to savage attacks. Three days later, Ambassador Grew again called upon the Japanese Foreign Minister Kōki Hirota, warning him of 'the very serious effect which would be produced in the United States … if some accident should occur in connection' with the Japanese navy's announced intention to bomb Nanking. Grew recalled that he employed the most emphatic language,

reminding Hirota that 'we must not forget history ... neither the American Government nor the American people had wanted war with Spain in 1898, but when the Maine was blown up nothing could prevent war.' Ambassador Grew feared that overeager Japanese aviators might attack a US ship or contingent of marines irrespective of restraining directives to exercise utmost caution. He blamed young, hot-headed Japanese aviators for causing trouble, commenting in his diary that 'having once smelled blood they simply fly amok and don't give a damn whom or what they hit.' Less than three months after warning Hirota that overeager Japanese aviators might plunge relations between the US and Japan into a crisis, Grew found himself issuing orders to the American embassy staff in Tokyo to begin planning for a hurried departure. The ambassador had received word that Japanese aircraft had sunk the USS *Panay* on 12 December as it lay at anchor upstream of Nanking.[1]

Japan may have said that this attack on the *Panay* was an accident but as any historian can see it was not, including Manny Koginos:

> Yet further evidence indicated otherwise; that the attack upon the American convoy was anything but a mistaken identity. Since December 11, 1937 an almost hourly account had been dispatched to the Japanese military and civilian authorities, both in Shanghai and Tokyo, announcing the changing positions of the Panay and its convoy. Even four hours' prior to the attack, the gunboat's nationality was made known to a Japanese military unit which halted the vessel before it had reached its fateful rendezvous point 27 miles above Nanking. Film taken on December 12 by a cameraman on board the Panay revealed a sunny cloudless day and it also showed American flags painted and displayed prominently on each of the vessels. It appears inconceivable that the Japanese pilots

could have failed to identify the nationality of the vessels at such low altitudes. Nor did the Japanese fully explain the assault upon the gunboat by a motor launch following the initial aerial attack and the subsequent aerial machine-gunning of the vessel's survivors as they attempted to escape to shore. Indeed, both the Japanese Army and Navy endeavored to minimize any direct responsibility for the attack, which explains the conflicting evidence reached in their respective investigations into the affair. Nor was American foreign policy substantially altered immediately following the Panay affair. The Panay incident simply reflected America's refusal to undertake a more aggressive program toward the Japanese. For the Japanese, the Panay incident was an obvious way station en route to Pearl Harbor.[2]

FDR had more than enough evidence after this attack to declare war on the Imperial Japanese Government, yet he would say to the American people that the *Panay* attack was just an accident, due to wreckless flying by the Japanese pilots. As anyone who has done some research in to this will know, this could no be further from the truth. It was a deliberate attack on a U.S. convoy that was being escorted by the *Panay*. The fact is that with all the information coming in from American intelligence in China and Japan this should have been a warning to the U.S. that Japan was not a friend to the American people and with the attack on the *Panay* this should have nailed the lid shut for FDR. Instead, he would allow Japan to commit atrocity after atrocity in China, Vietnam, and the Philippines through to the end of the war, when he could have declared war on Japan after the *Panay* incident. The thing that is so frightening here is that right after this the Nanking massacre took place. The fact that FDR could have possibly stopped this massacre by declaring war on Japan should bring up questions as to his ability to be the commander-in-chief of American forces during this time of crisis. Below is part of a document from the Library of Congress on the *Panay* incident which shows that FDR had no intention of declaring war on Japan at this time.

The Secretary of State to the Ambassador in Japan (Grew) on the Sinking of the USS Panay, telegram, Washington, 13 December 1937, 8 p.m.

Please communicate promptly to Hirota a note as follows: The Government and people of the United States have been deeply shocked by the facts of the bombardment and sinking of the U. S. S. Panay and the sinking or burning of the American steamers Meiping, Meian and Meisian [Meihsia] by Japanese aircraft.

The essential facts are that these American vessels were in the Yangtze River by uncontested and incontestable right; that they were flying the American flag; that they were engaged in their legitimate and appropriate business; that they were at the moment conveying American official and private personnel away from points where danger had developed; that they had several times changed their position, moving upriver, in order to avoid danger; and that they were attacked by Japanese bombing planes. With regard to the attack, a responsible Japanese naval officer at Shanghai has informed the Commander-in-Chief of the American Asiatic Fleet that the four vessels were proceeding upriver; that a Japanese plane endeavored to ascertain their nationality, flying at an altitude of three hundred meters, but was unable to distinguish the flags; that three Japanese bombing planes, six Japanese fighting planes, six Japanese bombing planes, and two Japanese bombing planes, in sequence, made attacks which resulted in the damaging of one of the American steamers, and the sinking of the U. S. S. Panay and the other two steamers.

Since the beginning of the present unfortunate hostilities between Japan and China, the Japanese Government and various

Japanese authorities at various points have repeatedly assured the Government and authorities of the United States that it is the intention and purpose of the Japanese Government and the Japanese armed forces to respect the rights and interests of other powers. On several occasions, however, acts of Japanese armed forces have violated the rights of the United States, have seriously endangered the lives of American nationals, and have destroyed American property. In several instances, the Japanese Government has admitted the facts, has expressed regrets, and has given assurances that every precaution will be taken against recurrence of such incidents. In the present case, acts of Japanese armed forces have taken place in complete disregard of American rights, have taken American life, and have destroyed American property both public and private.

In these circumstances, the Government of the United States requests and expects of the Japanese Government a formally recorded expression of regret, an undertaking to make complete and comprehensive indemnifications, and an assurance that definite and specific steps have been taken which will ensure that hereafter American nationals, interests and property in China will not be subjected to attack by Japanese armed forces or unlawful interference by any Japanese authorities or forces whatsoever.

Before seeing Hirota inform your British colleague of intended action and text, but do not thereafter await action by him.

We are informing British Government of this instruction to you.

HULL[3]

Research on the *Panay* incident should suggest that FDR's failure to take action against Japan for an unprovoked attack with the loss of American lives is a form of high treason. There was no excuse for FDR not to declare war on Japan after the sinking of the Panay.

FDR even had Alley the newsreel man delete 30ft of film that showed Japanese bombers shooting at the gunboat at deck level to cover up the attack.

What followed this attack in Nanking is one of the worst atrocities committed in the Second World War.

No one was spared by the Imperial Japanese Army during the Nanking Massacre (better known as the Rape of Nanking). It has been estimated by some scholars and historians that 100,000 to 300,000 women were raped and many murdered. This became national news in America, so there is no denying that President Roosevelt knew about these atrocities. Photographic evidence was smuggled out and placed in FDR's hands by mid-1938.

Again FDR would do nothing and blame public opinion as the reason why he did not take action. This is a fallacy for there were polls taken that indicated as many as 75 per cent of Americans were willing to go to war with Japan, just not Germany. The historian must remember that the United States was not practising isolationism in the Pacific, for the United States had military posts throughout the region: Hawaii, Philippines, Guam and gunboats in China, just to name a few. The concern for FDR was a third term as President of the United States, and he was more concerned about getting re-elected than doing the right thing. One other historical fact here is that over 90 per cent of United States veterans and military personnel and a huge population of the American public wanted to go to war with Japan after the sinking of the U.S. *Panay* in December 1937. So the argument of isolationism does not hold water in the Pacific War theatre. FDR's legacy should be one of failure to the American people.

Chapter VI

The Nanking Massacre, 1937–38

Readers should be advised this chapter contains graphic depictions of sexual violence.

The Nanking Massacre is often called the Forgotten Holocaust of the Second World War, and for good reason; it is. Very few people even know about this atrocity, and it is not taught in American public schools. Japan hides its true history and even teaches lies about history, so that we tend to forget what happened there. This becomes an atrocity in itself, for we forget the people who died and were murdered there. This was not war. War is not made upon women and children and babies, to kill them is cold-blooded murder. Also, these Japanese soldiers were not following the Bushido Code of the Samurai, for the Samurai Warrior would never have dishonoured himself in the way Japanese soldiers did in Nanking. So when Japanese historians say these soldiers were following the Bushido Code, it is total fabrication. The photos in this chapter will show that their actions were nothing more than cold-blooded murder. Plus, FDR knew this was going on from photos and information smuggled out to America by intelligence and clergy working in what was known as the safe zone, and he did nothing to try to stop it. Many Americans already knew the brutality of the Japanese soldier.

Philip Gavin is a historian in Japan who is trying to set the record straight by bringing out the truth of Japan's mass murders in the Nanking Massacre:

> In December of 1937, the Japanese Imperial Army marched into China's capital city of Nanking and proceeded to murder

300,000 out of 600,000 civilians and soldiers in the city. The actual military invasion of Nanking was preceded by a tough battle at Shanghai that began in the summer of 1937. Chinese forces there put up surprisingly stiff resistance against the Japanese Army, which had expected an easy victory in China. Unlike the troops at Shanghai, Chinese soldiers at Nanking were poorly led and loosely organized. After just four days of fighting, Japanese troops smashed into the city on December 13, 1937, with orders issued to 'kill all captives.'

Their first concern was to eliminate any threat from the 90,000 Chinese soldiers who surrendered. To the Japanese, surrender was an unthinkable act of cowardice and the ultimate violation of the rigid code of military honor. Throughout the city of Nanking, random acts of murder occurred as soldiers frequently fired their rifles into panicked crowds of civilians, killing indiscriminately. The incredible carnage – citywide burnings, stabbings, drowning, strangulations, rapes, thefts, and massive property destruction – continued unabated for about six weeks, from mid-December 1937 through the beginning of February 1938. After this period of unprecedented violence, the Japanese eased off somewhat and settled in for the duration of the war. To pacify the population during the long occupation, highly addictive narcotics, including opium and heroin, were distributed by Japanese soldiers to the people of Nanking, regardless of age. An estimated 50,000 persons became addicted to heroin while many others lost themselves in the city's opium dens. An extraordinary group of about 20 Americans and Europeans remaining in the city, composed of missionaries, doctors and businessmen, took it upon themselves to establish an International Safety Zone. On numerous occasions, they risked their lives by personally intervening to prevent the execution of Chinese men or the rape of women and young girls. These Westerners became the unsung heroes of Nanking.[1]

Japan could try and deny much of what happened in Nanking but one thing they could not deny was when an Imperial Japanese soldier from the Nanking Massacre returned to Japan and became a serial rapist and murderer through the acts he had learned in the Nanking Massacre. These atrocities he had committed in Nanking he would again commit on young Japanese girls in Tokyo after the war. He did this until he was finally tracked down by the police and brought to justice. However, there was no justice for the Chinese girls on whom he committed his atrocities. He got justice for the crimes he committed in Japan but not China. Japanese professor Katsuichi Honda reported in 2015:

> The soldier's name was Kodaira Yoshio, who testified at his trial before he was found guilty and executed. He said, 'When you're talking about the Japanese military, thievery, and rape just come with the territory. I used to do some pretty brutal things.'

He would go on to say this is what had spurred him into killing young Japanese girls once he returned to Japan and the war was over.

> Then there is the other case of a soldier that got away with the mass rape and murder in Nanking and would return to live in Japan and become a Medical Doctor. Nagatomi Hakudo readily admitted to exulting in killing from the first. His favorite form of killing was to behead his victims with his samurai sword. He admitted to the rape of over 20 females, many under the age of 16. He was never punished for his crimes, and admitted to killing over 200 Chinese prisoners.[2]

How could the United States government allow this man not to be brought to justice for his crimes? How is Ted Bundy, the mass murderer and rapist in the United States, different from Hakudo. The truth is he is not. It is unknown how many women Bundy raped and killed, yet here is a soldier who admitted to killing 200 Chinese. How could any military court not bring this war criminal to justice? The evidence was there to view for the courts and judges. However, much like FDR, they chose to ignore it.

Japanese historians who find the courage to write books about the Nanking Massacre/Rape of Nanking face unrelenting attacks. Two history professors at Waseda University, Hora Tomio and Honda Katsuichi, who investigated the Japanese atrocities in China, both came to the same conclusion that the Japanese Imperial Army killed over 300,000 people in Nanking between 1937 and 1938.[3]

The two Japanese officers who had staged the beheading contest were shot by firing squad, a soldier's death. They should have been hanged, for they were not soldiers in any sense.

This had to be the most evil atrocity that two Japanese soldiers made into a sport. The so-called 'Contest to Cut Down a Hundred' between two second lieutenants appeared in a series of articles printed in the *Tokyo Nichi Nichi Shimbun* newspaper in late 1937, detailing the supposed 'heroic' deeds of the contestants. Noda Tsuyoshi and Mukai Toshiaki, two second lieutenants, began a 'contest' to see who could kill 100 Chinese first. The newspaper reported the grisly affair as occurring in the thick of battle: As Second Lieutenant Mukai, who has reached the third *dan* in bayonet training, runs his fingers over the blade of "Seki-no-Magoroku," the sword at his side, Second Lieutenant Noda speaks of his treasured sword. On the day after their separate departures, Second Lieutenant Noda broke into an enemy pillbox and killed four enemy. Second Lieutenant Mukai invaded an enemy camp at Henglmzhen and laid fifty-five enemy low with his sword. The incident highlights the incredible levels of jingoism inculcated into the Japanese of the era by their government, and the underdevelopment of critical thinking skills even in those otherwise well-educated by Imperial universities. Most Japanese interpreted the contest as meaning the second lieutenants charged heroically in among the Chinese enemy and cut down dozens like action movie Samurai. No such action could in fact occur. The Nationalist soldiers, well-armed with high-powered rifles generally maintained better than their owners, would inevitably have killed a lone man with a sword attempting to close to melee range. Even if trained to standards inferior to those used for Japanese soldiers, the idea of a swordsman ploughing through trenches or camps filled with hostile riflemen and leaving 'red ruin' in his wake appears ludicrous and impossible. Noda himself scoffed at the notion when he spoke at the school in his hometown and frankly admitted to committing the mass murder of helpless prisoners. After declaring 'that stuff in the newspapers about the "brave warrior from the provinces" and the "brave warrior of contest to cut down a hundred," that's me,' he described how once a band of Chinese soldiers surrendered to the Japanese:

> We'd line them up and cut them down, from one end of the line to the other. I was praised for having killed a hundred people, but actually, almost all of them were killed in this way. The two of us did have a contest, but afterward, I was often asked whether it was a big deal and I said that it was no big deal.[4]

These two soldiers were mass murderers of Chinese, just to see who could win in a beheading contest. The thing to remember is that this was reported in a Japanese newspaper for the whole world to read, and for any historian to say that FDR did not have knowledge of this historical event, then he had not done his research for copies of this newspaper were delivered to the White House only a month after this historical event had happened.

FDR must have realised at this point, with the sinking of USS *Panay* and then the infamous Nanking Massacre, that there was no way to avoid a war with Imperial Japan. The information was right there in front of him to see and review from 1925 to 1937, and yet even when Americans were killed on the *Panay* the President refused to act. Mass murder in China was taking place on a huge scale and FDR with this information refusing to act is again high treason when Americans are killed. History needs to go back and review FDR and his policies.

The amazing thing is that FDR knew about all of this and did nothing. Then, of course, he would even cover up Japanese soldiers' atrocities committed on American soldiers on the Bataan Death March and the treatment of American prisoners of war held by the Japanese. In Germany, six out of ten American PoWs survived, but in Japan it was just one in ten.

The Nanking Massacre and Unit 731 were brutal and unfathomable, FDR knew about atrocities committed both by Germany and Japan yet did not attempt to stop them. The information was clearly there for him to see. Also, there were many Americans ready to go to war with Japan after the sinking of the *Panay*. Unlike Europe, the Pacific was not about isolationism, for America had soldiers and sailors in the Hawaiian Islands and the Philippines both located in the Pacific. This is also before Adolf Hitler and Germany had declared war on any country for that would not come until 1939. This cannot be an excuse for FDR to use to avoid a war against Japan.

How could a President of the United States cover up the *Panay* incident and the Nanking Massacre when all the information for it was public knowledge through the press and do nothing about it but allow it to continue. As a historian we must strive to bring out the truth about FDR, but instead many have acted much the same as FDR did; they cover up for him. If the United States had gone to war with Japan in 1937, the Bataan Death March would not have happened, Pearl Harbor would not have happened, Germany would have taken a back seat and the United States would have come into the war with Germany before December 1941. The war could have ended before 1945 and the use of the A-bomb. This could have all happened if FDR had declared war on Japan in 1937 for he had more than enough proof to give the American public as to why their country should go to war with Japan. The amount of American lives unnecessarily lost at Pearl Harbor and the Philippines is more than enough to prove FDR was guilty of treason. Instead many historians want to honor this man while they ignore the information that is out there on the many ways he failed as the President of the United States of America. He should be held accountable.

Chapter VII

Pearl Harbor Naval War Games Fleet Exercise XIX of 1938

The fact that these naval war games would result in the theoretical sinking of 98 per cent of the ships at Pearl Harbor should have sent up a red flag to any commander-in-chief like FDR. Again even the Navy and Army generals and admirals seemed to have had their heads buried in the sand after this exercise. The fact is the Japanese Navy's attack and operations plan was very similar to the U.S. Pacific Fleet's 1938 Fleet Exercise XIX in Hawaiian waters. This exercise consisted of a surprise air attack on Pearl Harbor by Navy aircraft from carriers, located in roughly the same position as the Japanese carriers on the morning of 7 December 1941. The Navy aircraft 'attacked' Navy and Army airfields on Oahu with 'devastating effect', which would have destroyed the ships and planes according to the Pacific Fleet's after-action report.

On 15 March 1938 the aircraft carrier USS *Saratoga*, CV3, sailed from San Diego for Fleet Problem XIX, again conducted off Hawaii. During the second phase of the problem, the aircraft carrier launched a surprise air attack on Pearl Harbor from a point 100 miles off Oahu, setting a pattern that the Japanese copied in December 1941. The Japanese spies at Pearl Harbor sent the information from the exercise to the Navy high command, giving them an excellent plan to conduct a surprise attack at Pearl Harbor. Among Admiral Ernest King's accomplishments was to corroborate Admiral Harry E. Yarnell's 1932 war game findings in 1938 by staging his own successful simulated naval air raid on Pearl Harbor, showing that the base was dangerously vulnerable to aerial attack. He was taken no more seriously than his contemporary until 7 December 1941, when the Imperial Japanese Navy attacked the base by air for real.

In searching the internet, National Archives and even the Library of Congress, the truly amazing thing is that almost all of the information on the Naval War Fleet Exercises of 1932 and 1938 are either classified or have disappeared completely, for through research one can find hardly any information on them. The after-action reports do not exist at any of these sites. The other problem when researching Admiral King is that although there is an abundance of material about him, there is very little on him and his Fleet Exercise XIX. In showing the weaknesses at Pearl Harbor, these after-action reports are highly essential. But where are these reports for the historian to use? Are they buried somewhere deep in Washington D.C. or have they been destroyed all together. That is a question that has to be asked.

Admiral King's Fleet Exercise XIX is the prime example of our commanders not taking heed of the weaknesses of Pearl Harbor's defences. It is also how Admiral Yamamoto, using Commander Minoru Genda, would devise his plan for an attack on Pearl Harbor. This would also prove to Admiral Richardson that the ships at Pearl Harbor were a sitting duck to an attack by the Japanese Imperial Navy. The mere fact that the supreme commanders of both the United States Army and Navy ignored this information shows the lacklustre leadership of FDR's commanders at this time when a war with Japan was inevitable. FDR again did nothing here to strengthen the defences at Pearl Harbor, but instead would make sanctions against the Imperial Japanese Government that would even push them faster into a war with the United States, although Japan had already as early as 1927 been planning for war. Again these Naval War Games of 1938 should have been FDR's wake-up call for what would happen at Pearl Harbor if the Japanese Navy did attack. Yet he and his commanders ignored them.

The information that is available on Fleet Exercise XIX (although not much) is that it was a rousing success in showing that Pearl Harbor could be attacked using aircraft carriers and that, with more than 98 per cent of the ships there destroyed and the airfields and the airplanes in the Hawaiian Islands totally destroyed, this Army and Navy base was a disaster waiting to happen in 1938. Of course, this disaster did happen on 7 December 1941 when Admiral Yamamoto's Pearl Harbor attack plan (which was based on Fleet Exercise XIX) lit up Pearl Harbor like a Christmas tree.

The question that any historian should ask here is why was this United States Navy war game ignored? It was already a major concern among high-ranking military members that war with Japan was coming. They had already attacked a Navy gunboat, the *Panay*, invaded China, and were making war throughout certain areas of the Pacific. The United States had an army in the Philippines under the command of General Douglas MacArthur that was poorly equipped for war and would have a hard time even defending the Philippines if it were to be attacked by Imperial Japan. The least FDR could have done was send military equipment there instead of Europe, for the soldiers were drilling with brooms as their rifles in the Philippines. Yet again FDR left American service men out to dry in the Philippines and Pearl Harbor. If he wanted to show Imperial Japan the weaknesses at Pearl Harbor and in the Philippines to get them to attack, then this certainly worked! The question is, 'Why FDR?' To the readers, sorry this was such a short chapter, but with there is very little information on Fleet Exercise XIX. The question is, 'Why?'

Chapter VIII

Warning to FDR by Admiral Richardson, October 1940

The question that any historian should ask here is 'Why would FDR ignore the evidence presented to him about the weakness of Pearl Harbor by a Fleet admiral in 1940, and then later relieve him of command?' Could it be that FDR was setting Pearl Harbor up for an attack by Japan? The answer has to be a resounding yes!

Admiral Richardson was one of the Navy's foremost figures. Since his earliest days, after leaving Annapolis, he had made himself one of the Navy's top admirals. In 1940, the policy-making branch of the Government in foreign affairs – the President and the Secretary of State – thought that stationing the Fleet in Hawaii would restrain the Japanese. They did not ask their senior military advisors whether it would accomplish such an end.

Richardson protested this redeployment to President Franklin D. Roosevelt and to others in Washington. He believed that advanced bases like Guam and Hawaii were necessary, but that insufficient funding and efforts had been made to prepare them to be used in wartime. He also believed future battles in the Pacific would involve aircraft carriers, and more scouting forces would be needed to locate them. Richardson recognized how vulnerable the Fleet was in such an exposed and remote position, a logistical nightmare that was only worsened by the slim resources and the lack of preparation and organization. It was Richardson's belief – and indeed generally supported by the Navy – that the Fleet should never be berthed inside Pearl Harbor where it would be a mark for attack. This was particularly true in such troubled times when the airways of the East were hot with rumors of approaching conflict. Richardson twice traveled to Washington to meet with Roosevelt to discuss the issue. He followed that up with an official letter to the Chief of Naval Operations (CNO), Admiral Harold R. Stark, pointing out his own firm conviction that neither the Navy nor the country was prepared for war with Japan. After his early October visit to Roosevelt, on October 26, 1940, a White House leak to the Washington-based *Kiplinger Newsletter* predicted that Richardson would be removed as fleet commander. Most believed he might be promoted upwards to replace Stark as CNO, but, instead he was fired.

Lieutenant Commander Arthur H. McCollum of Naval Intelligence was part of President Roosevelt's team that was working with FDR to get America into a war with Japan by making Japan attack the United States. Again the problem any historian should have with this is that FDR had more than enough reason to go to war with Japan when it attacked and sunk the *Panay* on the Yangtze River in China in 1937. The fact that FDR did not declare war on Imperial Japan after this is also ample reason he should have been charged with treason. McCollum should have also been charged with treason with the plan he came up with for FDR on October 1940.

'McCollum's 5 page memorandum of October 1940 ... put forward a startling plan – a plan intended to engineer a situation that would mobilize a reluctant America into joining Britain's struggle against the German armed forces then overrunning Europe. Its 8 actions called for virtually inciting a Japanese attack on American ground, air, and naval forces in Hawaii.'[1]

Again any historian doing research on this subject should realise that if America had gone to war with Japan in 1937 after the attack on the *Panay*, that the attack on Pearl Harbor and the Philippines would not have happened and the United States would have been in the war much sooner in Europe, possibly saving millions of lives in the process and keeping many of the atrocities of the Second World War from happening.

McCollum's code name was F-2 and he was essential to FDR's plan for war with Japan. All communications of intelligence on Japan went through McCollum to FDR from 1940 up to the attack on Pearl Harbor. This included decoded military reports destined for FDR and these came directly through the Far East Section of ONI, which McCollum oversaw. McCollum believed that war with Imperial Japan was inevitable. The eight actions that he presented to FDR in October 1940 were as follows:

1. Make arrangement with Britain for use of British bases in the Pacific, mainly Singapore.
2. Make arrangement with Holland for the use of base facilities and acquisition of supplies in the Dutch East Indies. (Indonesia)
3. Give all possible aid to the Chinese government of Chiang Kai-shek.
4. Send a division of long-range Navy heavy cruisers to the Orient, Philippines, or Singapore.
5. Send 2 divisions of submarines to the Orient.
6. Keep the main strength of the U.S. Fleet, now in the Pacific, in the Hawaiian Islands.
7. Insist that the Dutch refuse to grant Japanese demands for undue economic concessions, particularly oil.
8. Completely embargo all trade with Japan, in collaboration with a similar embargo imposed by the British Empire.[2]

Although this memo was sent to FDR's most trusted Navy military advisor, Captain Dudley Knox, and Knox endorsed the memo, the paper trail ends with him, allowing historians/scholars to deny FDR ever got the memo. This is hogwash for Knox would have given the memo to FDR, for it was written for the President. FDR got the memo and destroyed it so it could not be traced back to him. This happened right after the attack on Pearl Harbor (the next day) with hundreds of other documents that FDR did not want to be seen.

The very next day after Knox endorsed the plan, McCollum's proposals went into effect. The most shocking part of one of McCollum's proposals to FDR was Action D. This could have got even more men killed than the later attack on Pearl Harbor. This was the deliberate deployment of American warships within the territorial waters of Japan. During secret Whitehouse meetings, FDR took charge of Action D. FDR said 'I just want our ships to keep popping up here and there and keep the Japanese guessing. I do not mind losing one or two cruisers.'[3]

Admirals Kimmel and Richardson were against Action D. Any historian who promotes the idea that FDR would not sacrifice the men at Pearl Harbor either has not done his research or is helping cover up FDR's actions for he had no problem in sacrificing soldiers and sailors lives in Action D, as FDR's statement shows. Again FDR should have been charged with treason for sending these ships into Japanese-held waters.

After this memo came out Americans were told by FDR to get out of countries in the Far East, except the Hawaiian Islands and the Philippines. Most of the Navy commanders would not stand up to FDR but Admiral Richardson would and did. The one thing that historians should get straight is that men such as General 'Billy' Mitchell and Admiral James O. Richardson were heroes to the American people by speaking their minds and telling the top brass that their actions were foolhardy. Furthermore, they said, it would cost American soldiers and sailors their lives if these policies were not changed.

All any historian would have to do to check on Action D is to visit the Library of Congress, because the information of corruption is right there to find. FDR liked to call them 'Pop-Up Cruises', which led American sailors into Harm's Way. 'From March through July 1941, White House records show that FDR ignored International Law and dispatched naval task groups into Japanese waters on 3 such pop-up cruises.'[4]

These cruises are documented, with the first one in March 1941 led by Vice Admiral John H. Newton. The task group consisted of four heavy cruisers; they were the USS *Brooklyn*, USS *Chicago*, USS *Savannah* and USS *Portland*, and there were twelve destroyers in the task group. It is clear that FDR wanted this task group to be attacked and destroyed, with the death of thousands of sailors. This information was to be kept top secret. However, after the end of the war, Admiral Newton testified at the Hart Investigation into Pearl Harbor that his orders were highly secret and given to him verbally (PHPT 26-340 in the Library of Congress). This information was leaked out by an Australian newspaper in an effort to get Japan to attack, so to FDR it was not top secret but it was told to the Admiral Newton that it was top secret. The Foreign Minister of Japan, Yosuke Matsuoka, was made aware of this task group, so Japan knew it was in Japan's waters.

The most dangerous Action D pop-up cruise was the one that went into the Bungo Strait on 31 July 1941. The strait lies south-east of Honshu, which leads to the Inland Sea of Japan and is is dangerously close to Kyushu and Shikoku, was an area of operations for warships of the Imperial Japanese Navy during this time. There was a formal protest registered with Ambassador Joseph Grew in Tokyo that read: 'On the night of July 31st, 1941 Japanese Fleet units at anchor in Sukumo Bay picked up the sound of propellers approaching Bungo Channel from the eastward; Duty destroyers of the Japanese navy investigated and sighted two darkened cruisers that disappeared in a southerly direction behind a smoke screen when they were challenged. Japan naval officers believed the vessels were United States cruisers.'[5] A copy of this protest was forwarded to FDR. One can assume that FDR got a laugh out of it, for he was trying to incite Japan into attacking these cruisers so America could declare war as early as August 1941.

The amazing thing is that the name of the two cruisers that went into the Bungo Strait of the United States remains top secret or the files have been destroyed, for as of today, the American public does not know the name of these vessels and information about the incursion was not even released until late 1995. The officers and sailors on these ships were sworn to secrecy and now with few war veterans still alive, the American public may never know the cruisers' identities. The deck logs of the other two task groups are all blacked out in the National Archives and the commander's log of each of the ships in the first two pop-up cruises of Action D are also all blacked out, so no historian can research them to gain any information the crew of these ships might have known.

FDR did not care about American lives, he only cared about his political career, which seems today as that of a dictator since he was elected president four times and if he lived he may have campaigned for the presidency again in 1948. The thing we do know now about FDR is that he sacrificed American soldiers and sailors lives for no other reason other than to draw the United States into a war with Japan, a war that should have been declared in December 1937 with the sinking of the USS *Panay* on the Yangtze.

The one admiral who had the courage to stand up to FDR was Admiral James Richardson. The thing that really made Richardson explode against FDR was that the President was ordering the United States Navy Fleet based in Hawaii to stay put under Action F but was telling all Americans to leave any other Far Eastern country after the McCollum memo came to him. FDR's argument was that the US an army in the Philippines and they would also stay put like the Navy at Pearl Harbor.

In October 1940 and then again in January 1941 Richardson told FDR, 'Mr. President, senior officers of the Navy do not have the trust and confidence in the civilian leadership of this country that is essential for the successful prosecution of a war in the Pacific.' Richardson knew that this was placing the fleet in Hawaii in grave danger. Richardson disagreed with FDR completely over the fact that the President was willing to sacrifice a ship of the U.S. Navy to incite a war with Japan and the fact that FDR said, 'Sooner or later the Japanese would commit an overt act against the United States and the nation would be willing to enter the war.'[6] FDR must have forgotten the fact that Japan had already done this with the *Panay* attack and he did nothing. Again he was more concerned with his political career than the American people. Richardson's main concern was for his men and warships, and FDR's policy was not something to be taken lightly.

FDR relieved Richardson of command in February of 1941 and replaced him with Rear Admiral Husband Kimmel, promoting him to full admiral, for Kimmel was a yes man and would do whatever FDR asked. Many people were apprised of an attack that was coming to

Pearl Harbor and one was General Douglas MacArthur. He received the order from President Roosevelt to stand aside; just remain in a defensive posture and let Japan commit the first overt act of war. And that's what he did. And he replied to the order by saying that everything was ready for a successful defence. Admiral Hart, who was the commander of the U.S. Asiatic Fleet, got that order, and he ordered all of his submarines to submerge in Manila Bay instead of attacking Japanese troop ships that were coming in and invading the Philippines. So the whole idea was to follow the order and let Japan commit the first overt act of war. And MacArthur, beginning on 3 December 1941, started a rushed airstrip in Mindanao in the southernmost part of the Philippines, so that he could escape by B-17, and he took his key staff members, including his cryptologist and the radio people that was supplying this information with him but he left General Jonathan Wainwright at Bataan, and any historian knows what happened at Bataan.

Admiral Richardson knew that Pearl Harbor was a sitting duck for an attack by the Imperial Japanese Navy and pointed this out quite clearly to President Roosevelt. This was a U.S. Navy Fleet Admiral who understood the Japanese better than anyone on FDR's staff and yet the President would not take his advice. The question is why and the answer is simple: FDR wanted to get into a war with Japan and he did not care how many American lives he had to sacrifice to get there. This again brings up the idea of charges that should have been levelled against FDR for treason. FDR set up the attack on for Pearl Harbor and the Philippines knowing it would cost thousands of American soldiers and sailors their lives, and many of his commanders knew this. General George C. Marshall said to his subordinate officers of this information on Pearl Harbor, 'We will have to take it to the grave with us gentlemen.' A historian must wonder what other information is out there that is hidden from the American public that is still classified as Top Secret or has been destroyed or blacked out when given to the Library of Congress and the National Archives.

Warning to FDR by Admiral Richardson, October 1940

OP-16-F-2   ONI   7 October 1940

MEMORANDUM FOR THE DIRECTOR

SUBJECT: Estimate of the Situation in the Pacific and Recommendations for Action by the United States.

1. The United States today finds herself confronted by a hostile Germany and Italy in Europe and by an equally hostile Japan in the Orient. Russia, the great land link between these two groups of hostile powers, is at present neutral, but in all probability favorably inclined towards the Axis powers, and her favorable attitude towards these powers may be expected to increase in direct proportion to increasing success in their prosecution of the war in Europe. Germany and Italy have been successful in war on the continent of Europe and all of Europe is either under their military control or has been forced into subservience. Only the British Empire is actively opposing by war the growing world dominance of Germany and Italy and their satellites.

2. The United States at first remained coolly aloof from the conflict in Europe and there is considerable evidence to support the view that Germany and Italy attempted by every method within their power to foster a continuation of American indifference to the outcome of the struggle in Europe. Paradoxically, every success of German and Italian arms has led to further increases in United States sympathy for and material support of the British Empire, until at the present time the United States government stands committed to a policy of rendering every support short of war with the chances rapidly increasing that the United States will become a full fledged ally of the British Empire in the very near future. The final failure of German and Italian diplomacy to keep the United States in the role of a disinterested spectator has forced them to adopt the policy of developing threats to U.S. security in other spheres of the world, notably by the threat of revolutions in South and Central America by Axis-dominated groups and by the stimulation of Japan to further aggressions and threats in the Far East in the hope that by these means the United States would become so confused in thought and fearful of her own immediate security as to cause her to become so preoccupied in purely defensive preparations as to virtually preclude U.S. aid to Great Britain in any form. As a result of this policy, Germany and Italy have lately concluded a military alliance with Japan directed against the United States. If the published terms of this treaty and the pointed utterances of German, Italian and Japanese leaders can be believed, and there seems no ground on which to doubt either, the three totalitarian powers agree to make war on the United States, should she come to the assistance of England, or should she attempt to forcibly interfere with Japan's aims in the Orient and,

Part of a copy of the McCollum memo for FDR on how to start a war with Japan.

Chapter IX

Japan 1940 Onward/FDR's Secret Ways to Get Japan in the War

FDR was searching for many ways to get Japan to attack America. In the previous chapter it was shown how FDR had set up Pearl Harbor and the Philippines for an attack as well as trying to incite the Japanese into attacking US Navy ships with Action D. Yet Roosevelt would use other ways to entice Japan into war. One was to tighten the control on trade with Japan. American was warned, however, that an attack Pearl Harbor was likely if Japan went to war with the United States.

Beginning in 1938, the U.S. adopted a succession of increasingly restrictive trade restrictions with Japan. This included terminating its 1911 commercial treaty in 1939, further tightened by the Export Control Act of 1940. These efforts failed to deter Japan from continuing its war in China, or from signing the Tripartite Pact in 1940 with Nazi Germany and Fascist Italy, officially forming the Axis.

After January 1940, the United States combined a strategy of increasing aid to China through larger credits and the Lend-Lease programme with a gradual move towards an embargo on the trade of all militarily useful items with Japan. The Japanese Government made several decisions during these two years that exacerbated the situation. Unable or unwilling to control the military, Japan's political leaders sought greater security by establishing the 'Greater East Asia Co-Prosperity Sphere' in August 1940. In so doing they announced Japan's intention to drive the Western imperialist nations from Asia. However, this Japanese-led project aimed to enhance Japan's

Avenge Pearl Harbor World War II poster circulated in the USA after the attack on Pearl Harbor.

On December 12, 1937 Japanese planes bombed a US river gunboat, the Panay, in China. The Panay sank, 2 were killed and 30 wounded. Panay hero receives Navy Cross. Washington, D.C., July 1. Fireman first class John L. Hodge, who is recuperating at Naval Hospital here, was today decorated with the Navy Cross for the bravery he displayed during the sinking of the U.S. gunboat Panay by Japanese bombs last year. Assistant Secretary of the Navy Charles Edison is pictured pinning the award on the Bluejacket. It was Hodge who carried Jim Marshall, staff writer for Collier's injured in the bombing, from the scene of the sinking vessel to Wuhu, China, a distance of about 17 miles, 7/1/38."[5] FDR even had Alley the Newsreel man to delete 30 ft. of film that showed Japanese bombers shooting at the gunboat at deck level to cover up the attack.

Japanese Admiral Isoroku Yamamoto Commander in Chief, Combined Fleet conceived the Pearl Harbor Attack.

Franklin D Roosevelt, General McArthur and Admiral Nimitz in Pearl Harbor, Hawaii.

The Pearl Harbor National Memorial in Honolulu, Hawaii. © Gage Skidmore.

Japanese Navy Aichi D3A1 Type 99 carrier bombers (allied codename *Val*) prepare to take off from an aircraft carrier during the morning of 7 December 1941. Ship in the background is the carrier *Soryu* (7 December 1941).

Attack on the USS *West Virginia*.

Battleship Row during the attack.

Airfield bomb by the Imperial Japan Navy.

The USS West Virginia, left, was one of the battleships to sink during the attack.

USS *West Virginia* and The USS *Tennessee*.

The carnage was complete.

The USS *Arizona* going down.

The USS *Shaw* exploded during the attack.

economic and material wealth so that it would not be dependent upon supplies from the West, and not to 'liberate' the long-subject peoples of Asia. In fact, Japan would have to launch a campaign of military conquest and rule, and did not intend to pull out of China. At the same time, several pacts with Western nations only made Japan appear more of a threat to the United States. First, Japan signed the Tripartite Pact with Germany and Italy on 27 September 1940 and thereby linked the conflicts in Europe and Asia. This made China a potential ally in the global fight against fascism. Then in mid-1941, Japan signed a Neutrality Pact with the Soviet Union, making it clear that Japan's military would be moving into Southeast Asia, where the United States had greater interests. A third agreement with Vichy France enabled Japanese forces to move into Indochina and begin their southern advance. The United States responded to this growing threat by temporarily halting negotiations with Japanese diplomats, instituting a full embargo on exports to Japan, freezing Japanese assets in U.S. banks, and sending supplies into China along the Burma Road. Although negotiations restarted after the United States increasingly enforced an embargo against Japan, they made little headway. Diplomats in Washington came close to agreements on a couple of occasions, but pro-Chinese sentiment in the United States made it difficult to reach any resolution that would not involve a Japanese withdrawal from China, and such a condition was unacceptable to Japan's military leaders.

Faced with serious shortages as a result of the embargo, unable to retreat, and convinced that U.S. officials opposed further negotiation, Japan's leaders came to the conclusion that they had to act swiftly. For their part, U.S. leaders had not given up on a negotiated settlement. This was a sure-fire way to get Japan into war.

On 26 November 1941 Secretary of State Hull presented 'peace terms' to the Japanese. These were such that in order for Japan to agree to them they would have had to withdraw from China, and essentially end all hostilities, something that the administration knew was not going to happen. Hull's oral presentation to the Japanese was as follows:

> The representatives of the Government of the United States and of the Government of Japan have been carrying on during the past several months informal and exploratory conversations for the purpose of arriving at a settlement if possible of questions relating to the entire Pacific area based upon the principles of peace, law and order and fair dealing among nations.
>
> These principles include the principle of inviolability of territorial integrity and sovereignty of each and all nations; the principle of non-interference in the internal affairs of other countries; the principle of equality, including equality of commercial opportunity and treatment; and the principle of reliance upon international cooperation and conciliation for the prevention and pacific settlement of controversies and for improvement of international conditions by peaceful methods and processes. It is believed that in our discussions some progress has been made in reference to the general principles which constitute the basis of a peaceful settlement covering the entire Pacific area. Recently the Japanese Ambassador has stated that the Japanese Government is desirous of continuing the conversations directed toward a comprehensive and peaceful settlement of the Pacific area; that it would be helpful toward creating an atmosphere favorable to the successful outcome of the conversations if a temporary modus vivendi could be agreed upon to be in effect while the conversations looking to peaceful settlement in the Pacific were continuing.
>
> On November 20 the Japanese Ambassador communicated to the Secretary of State proposals in regard to temporary measures to be taken respectively by the Government of Japan and by the Government of the United States, which measures are understood to have been designed to accomplish

the purposes above indicated. The Government of the United States most earnestly desires to contribute to the promotion and maintenance of peace and stability in the Pacific area, and to afford every opportunity for the continuance of discussion with the Japanese Government directed toward working out a broad-gauge program of peace throughout the Pacific area. The proposals which were presented by the Japanese Ambassador on November 20 contain some features which, in the opinion of this Government, conflict with the fundamental principles which form a part of the general settlement under consideration and to which each Government has declared that it is committed. The Government of the United States believes that the adoption of such proposals would not be likely to contribute to the ultimate objectives of ensuring peace under law, order and justice in the Pacific area, and it suggests that further effort be made to resolve our divergences of view in regard to the practical application of the fundamental principles already mentioned. With this object in view the Government of the United States offers for the consideration of the Japanese Government a plan of a broad but simple settlement covering the entire Pacific area as one practical exemplification of a program which this Government envisages as something to be worked out during our further conversations.

The plan therein suggested represents an effort to bridge the gap between our draft of June 21, 1941 and the Japanese draft of September 25 by making a new approach to the essential problems underlying a comprehensive Pacific settlement. This plan contains provisions dealing with the practical application of the fundamental principles which we have agreed in our conversations constitute the only sound basis for worthwhile international relations. We hope that in this way progress toward reaching a meeting of minds between our two Governments may be expedited.

The text of the Hull memo is below:

November 26, 1941
Outline of Proposed Basis for Agreement Between the United States and Japan
Section I
Draft Mutual Declaration of Policy
The Government of the United States and the Government of Japan both being solicitous for the peace of the Pacific affirm that their national policies are directed toward lasting and extensive peace throughout the Pacific area, that they have no territorial designs in that area, that they have no intention of threatening other countries or of using military force aggressively against any neighboring nation, and that, accordingly, in their national policies they will actively support and give practical application to the following fundamental principles upon which their relations with each other and with all other governments are based: The principle of inviolability of territorial integrity and sovereignty of each and all nations: The principle of non-interference in the internal affairs of other countries: The principle of equality, including equality of commercial opportunity and treatment: The principle of reliance upon international cooperation and conciliation for the prevention and pacific settlement of controversies and for improvement of international conditions by peaceful methods and processes.

The Government of Japan and the Government of the United States have agreed that toward eliminating chronic political instability, preventing recurrent economic collapse, and providing a basis for peace, they will actively support and practically apply the following principles in their economic relations with each other and with other nations and peoples: The principle of non-discrimination in international commercial relations: The principle of international economic cooperation and abolition of extreme nationalism as expressed in excessive trade restrictions: The principle of non-discriminatory access by all nations to raw material supplies: The principle of full protection of the interests of consuming countries and populations as regards the operation of international commodity agreements: The principle of establishment of such institutions and arrangements of international finance as may lend aid to the essential enterprises and the continuous development of all countries and may permit payments through processes of trade consonant with the welfare of all countries.

Section II
Steps To Be Taken by the Government of the United States and by the Government of Japan
The Government of the United States and the Government of Japan propose to take steps as follows: The Government of the United States and the Government of Japan will endeavor to conclude a multilateral non-aggression pact among the British Empire, China, Japan, the Netherlands, the Soviet Union, Thailand and the United States.

These Governments will endeavor to conclude among the American, British, Chinese, Japanese, the Netherlands and Thai Governments that they will pledge themselves to respect the territorial integrity of French Indochina and, in the event that there should develop a threat to the territorial integrity of Indochina, to enter into immediate consultation with a view to taking such measures as may be deemed necessary and advisable to meet the threat in question. Such agreement would provide also that each of the Governments party to the agreement would not seek or accept preferential treatment in its trade or economic relations with Indochina and would use its influence to obtain for each of the signatories equality of treatment in trade and commerce with French Indochina.

The Government of Japan will withdraw all military, naval, air and police forces from China and from Indochina: The Government of the United States and the Government of Japan will not support – militarily, politically economically – any government or regime in China other than the National Government of the Republic of China with capital temporarily at Chungking. Both Governments will endeavor to obtain the agreement of the British and other governments to give up extraterritorial rights in China, including rights in international settlements and in concessions and under the Boxer Protocol of 1901.

The Government of the United States and the Government of Japan will enter into negotiations for the conclusion between the United States and Japan of a trade agreement, based upon reciprocal most favored-nation treatment and reduction of trade barriers by both countries, including an undertaking by the United States to bind raw silk on the free list. The Government of the United States and the Government of Japan will, respectively, remove the freezing restrictions on Japanese funds in the United States and on American funds in Japan.

Both Governments will agree upon a plan for the stabilization of the dollar-yen rate, with the allocation of funds adequate for this purpose, half to be supplied by Japan and half by the United States. Both Governments will agree that no agreement which either has concluded with any third power or powers shall be interpreted by it in such a way as to conflict with the fundamental purpose of this agreement, the establishment and preservation of peace throughout the Pacific area. Both Governments will use their influence to cause other governments to adhere to and to give practical application to the basic political and economic principles set forth in this agreement.

In the American climate at the time FDR knew that it would not be possible for him to get the U.S. to enter the war unless it was attacked.

Again, it had already been in the *Panay* incident. Ever since the war Americans have generally believed, because that is what they were told to believe, that America was just peacefully minding its own business when Japan, for no reason at all other than their own aggression, came out of nowhere to attack America. In other words, that America was an 'innocent victim'. This is not the case, though. The Japanese were being provoked and baited by the FDR administration to attack America in the Pacific. History is not being rewritten, these are the facts. FDR would incite Japan into a war with America. However, as in the previous chapters it was shown that America should have already been in a war as far back as 1937. It is amazing how even back then members of FDR's staff were doing their best to cover up the fact that he was doing everything in his power to ignite a full-scale war with the Imperial Japanese Government.

On 24 July 1941 Tokyo decided to strengthen its position in terms of its invasion of China by moving through Southeast Asia. Given that France had long occupied parts of the region, and Germany, a Japanese ally, now controlled most of France through Petain's puppet government, France 'agreed' to the occupation of its Indo-China colonies. Japan followed up by occupying Cam Ranh naval base, 800 miles from the Philippines, where America had troops, and the British base at Singapore in February 1942.

On 26 July, President Roosevelt swung into action by freezing all Japanese assets in America. Britain and the Dutch East Indies followed suit. The result: Japan lost access to three quarters of its overseas trade and 88 per cent of its imported oil. Japan's oil reserves were only sufficient to last three years, and only half that time if it went to war and consumed fuel at a more frenzied pace. Japan's immediate response was to occupy Saigon, again with Vichy France's acquiescence. If Japan could gain control of Southeast Asia, including Malaya, it could also control the region's rubber and tin production – a serious blow to the West, which imported such materials from the East. Japan was now faced with a dilemma: back off of its occupation of Southeast Asia and hope the oil embargo would be eased – or seize the oil and further antagonise the West, even into war.

The United States did not have to provoke Japan into war, it had already been planned back in 1927 with the Tanaka Memorial. In early January 1941 Admiral Yamamoto's Pearl Harbor attack plan had already been leaked to the United States Embassy in Tokyo. The leak was to Max Bishop, the Third Secretary at the embassy. It came from the Peruvian Minister to Japan, Dr Ricardo Rivera Schreiber, while they were making transactions at a bank in Tokyo on 26 January 1941. Pulling Bishop to the side, Schreiber told him that if trouble with the United States came, Japanese military forces were planning to attempt a massive surprise attack on Pearl Harbor using all of their military resources. This information was presented to Ambassador Joseph Grew, who at 6 p.m. Japan time send an encrypted dispatch to Secretary of State Cordell Hull. Hull read the message on 27 January 1941. It read:

MY PERUVIAN COLLEAGUE TOLD A MEMBER OF MY STAFF THAT HE HAD HEARD FROM MANY SOURCES INCLUDING A JAPANESE SOURCE THAT THE JAPANESE MILITARY FORCES PLANNED IN THE EVENT OF TROUBLE WITH THE UNITED STATES, TO ATTEMPT A SURPRISE ATTACK ON PEARL HARBOR USING ALL THEIR MILITARY FACILITIES. HE ADDED THAT ALTHOUGH THE PROJECT SEEMED FANTASTIC THE FACT THAT HE HEARD IT FROM MANY SOURCES PROMPTED HIM TO PASS THE INFORMATION. GREW.[2]

Copies of this memo were sent to Army and Navy Intelligence as well as to President Roosevelt. This information was just what FDR wanted to hear. A surprise attack by the Japanese on Pearl Harbor would ignite the American people into war, but it must be seen as a surprise attack. Again it did not matter if FDR enticed Japan into war it was already

Japan 1940 Onward/FDR's Secret Ways to Get Japan in the War 127

in their plan. The fact that every major commander knew that Pearl Harbor was a sitting duck for an attack by Japan proves that FDR knew this would entail a major loss of life of American soldiers and sailors. Then, of course, FDR knew it would only be a matter of time before Japan would attack and invade the Philippine Islands. For the atrocities committed in the Philippines by the Japanese, the blame should also be put on FDR, for instead of sending military supplies to Europe he could have armed the U.S. Military at the Philippines to the teeth to the point where no attempted Japanese invasion would have been successful. The fact that FDR knew the attack was coming and he did nothing to improve the defenses of the Hawaii Islands or the Philippines and allowed all of these lives to be ended for no other reason than to get the US into a war with Imperial Japan shows that the President was guilty of treason against the United States as well as humanity. Historians and scholars who defend FDR and these actions today are doing nothing more than lying about history.

128 FDR and High Treason at Pearl Harbor

```
NAVAL MESSAGE                              NAVY DEPARTMENT
             Op-12 Ext. 2992                         MESSAGE
PHONE EXTENSION NUMBER        ADDRESSEES            PRECEDENCE
FROM  Chief of Naval Operations    CINCAF      PRIORITY   X
RELEASED BY                        CINCPAC     ROUTINE
DATE   November 27, 1941                       DEFERRED

TOR CODEROOM                       CINCLANT    PRIORITY
DECODED BY                         SPENAVO     ROUTINE
                                               DEFERRED
PARAPHRASED BY
INDICATE BY ASTERISK ADDRESSEES FOR WHICH MAIL DELIVERY IS SATISFACTORY
```

GKVJL BVKLW 272337   0971

THIS DESPATCH IS TO BE CONSIDERED A WAR WARNING X NEGOTIATIONS WITH JAPAN LOOKING TOWARD STABILIZATION OF CONDITIONS IN THE PACIFIC HAVE CEASED AND AN AGGRESSIVE MOVE BY JAPAN IS EXPECTED WITHIN THE NEXT FEW DAYS X THE NUMBER AND EQUIPMENT OF JAPANESE TROOPS AND THE ORGANIZATION OF NAVAL TASK FORCES INDICATES AN AMPHIBIOUS EXPEDITION AGAINST EITHER THE PHILIPPINES THAI OR KRA PENINSULA OR POSSIBLY BORNEO X EXECUTE AN APPROPRIATE DEFENSIVE DEPLOYMENT PREPARATORY TO CARRYING OUT THE TASKS ASSIGNED IN WPL46X INFORM DISTRICT AND ARMY AUTHORITIES X A SIMILAR WARNING IS BEING SENT BY WAR DEPARTMENT X SPENAVO INFORM BRITISH X

SECRET

ORIGINAL ONLY DELIVER TO COMMUNICATION WATCH OFFICER IN PERSON

This document was a way to leave Pearl Harbor open for an attack by the Japanese. Admiral Richardson knew that Pearl Harbor was no place for the American Fleet.[3]

The other problem any historian should have in trying to defend FDR is that he pushed Japan beyond the limit when he put the trade embargoes in full force. This only led Japan to attack the United States sooner rather than later. There is no doubt that war was coming with Japan, for it had been set into motion back in 1927, as the Tanaka Memorial had presented with complete clarity. In the summer of 1941 it was clear to anyone in FDR's staff that Japan was going to attack the United States and these embargoes forced Japan to act quickly. The fact that FDR seized all of Japan's assets in the United States was a calling card that he wanted a war with Japan.

Any historian should also remember than in 1940 a deal that allowed the sale of millions of gallons of petroleum products to Japan came to an end in 1941, with all trade with Japan being embargoed. At this recourse Japan decided to go to war with the United States as soon as possible. Cutting off Japan's money, fuel and trade made the people living in the Hawaiian Islands cringe so much so that on 25 July 1941 the *Honolulu Advertiser* published a story about a possible air attack from Japan on Pearl Harbor. The point here is quite clear that FDR was pushing Japan into war without any concern for the United States' Naval and Army bases at Pearl Harbor and was leaving them vulnerable to an attack from Japan. And it must be pointed out again that yes America wanted isolation from an European war, but this did not entail isolation from conflict in the Pacific, for American servicemen were stationed throughout the region, not just in Hawaii and the Philippines, but on smaller islands like Guam that could also come under attack from Japan. FDR put countless American lives at risk by not providing supplies to the Pacific stations but instead sending these military supplies to Europe. This along with FDR's reluctant actions involving the sinking of USS *Panay* makes him guilty of treason, as any historian should be aware.

Chapter X

Breaking Japan's Codes

Another advantage FDR had over Japan was that in late 1939 America had put together a team of experts to break Japanese code messages coming across the wire.

If one seeks the truth, then one must realize just how corrupt FDR was at the time, and any information that would show that he knew Pearl Harbor was going to be attacked by Japan on 7 December 1941 would have been destroyed. There is no way any historian should buy into the fact that America did not know that Japan was going to attack Pearl Harbor since this is what FDR was pushing for.

Those documents that have not been destroyed or hidden away due to national security can be found in the Library of Congress or the National Archives if the historian or journalist does his or her research and finds them. Journalists who write protecting fake history, and who have never served this country in the military, do their best to discredit Robert Stinnett, who was a Naval officer in the Second World War and claim that his best-selling book, *Day of Deceit*, did not tell the truth. They did not cover in their books the actual history, neither of the naval war games of 1932 or 1938 that each sunk over 95 per cent of the Navy ships at Pearl Harbor, nor did they discuss the question that all Japanese naval cadets had to answer to graduate from 1935 to December 1941, 'How would you conduct a surprise attack on Pearl Harbor', nor do they discuss the sinking of USS *Panay*, the Nanking Massacre and the fact that FDR knew all about these incidents.

Much like the nineteenth-century military philosopher Carl von Clausewitz wrote, 'they invent history instead of telling the truth'. They are the scholars and historians who try to say that the Tanaka Memorial was a Russian plant, which is completely bogus as proven by Russian historian Leon Trotsky, and more scholars of this historical evidence are now saying it is real. So Mr Stinnett (RIP), any historian should salute you. Mr Stinnett has been praised for his work by numerous individuals around the world. The truth of history always comes out no matter who tries to cover it up. Journalists do their best to cover up the truth about Pearl Harbor.

This here is a prime example of how information about Pearl Harbor is still covered up today. The Japanese carrier *Akagi* and the entire operation of Japan's carrier force was under scrutiny by six U.S. Navy stations from August 1941 right up to the attack on Pearl Harbor. Robert Ogg, an officer in Naval Intelligence at the time, reported this and he is backed up by the document HYOO 8. This document identifies the six Navy stations. One is Station TARE, which is at Point St George in northern California and another was Station X, not the real name because it was classified as 'Top Secret' by the United States government. However, it was declassified in 2021 and was identified by Ogg and U.S. Navy records as the British-owned radio facility of Mackay Radio and Telegraph on the San Francisco peninsula near Half Moon Bay, California. The Mackay radio call letters were KFS.

Also it must be remembered that three Naval officers who were colleagues of Ogg in Naval Intelligence confirmed that he was involved in gathering Japanese naval intelligence for the U.S. Navy. They are all retired and now dead and cannot defend themselves. They were Commander Charles Black, Lt Commander William Barkan and Captain James McCollum. Black reported that they all were aware that U.S. Navy radio cryptographers were breaking into the Japanese codes and communications. Barkan even said that Washington D.C. knew what was going on. They went undercover as U.S. Customs officers and boarded Japanese vessels and got the codes. There were no Japanese codes that were not broken. This allowed United States Naval Intelligence to know what the Japanese Navy was doing at any time.

To say that FDR and United States military intelligence did not know what was going on is just a lie no matter how anyone cuts it.

American cryptographers knew the Japanese code techniques by heart because they had already solved the J series in the 1920s. Then of course in 1941, Japan thought that they would outsmart the United States code-breakers by introducing new minor variants into their codes every three months. The amazing thing is just how stupid the Japanese were because the code series they would put into effect in 1941 was read and decoded within a single day, so claims that FDR did not know what was going on in the Pacific are down to journalists and scholars covering up for the President's crimes, because when you allow American soldiers and sailors to be murdered just to get you into a war, that is high treason.

'The most explosive controversy involving America's foreknowledge of Japan's attack on Pearl Harbor centers on the Kaigun Ango (Navy Code), a system of 29 separate naval codes. Japan used 4 of these systems to organize and dispatch her warships to Hawaii by radio. America's 'splendid arrangement' had solved each of the 4 by the fall of 1941. So had the British, the Dutch, and the Chinese government of Chiang Kai-shek. An 80-year cover-up has hidden American and Allied success in obtaining the solutions to the Kaigun Ango prior to Pearl Harbor. American Naval Officers hid key code documents from congressional investigators. Naval Intelligence records, deceptively altered, were placed in the U.S. Navy's cryptology files to hide the cryptographic success. Many of these files have been destroyed or lost from the Library of Congress/National Archives. The 4 primary systems were: (1) Code Book D, known to American cryptographers as the 5-Num code; (2) a radio call sign code assigned to Japanese officials, shore stations, warships, and Marus; (3) the Ship Movement code, a system for reporting arrival and departures of naval vessels from Japanese ports and anchorages, known to Americans as the SM Code; (4) the Shin Code, used for contacting vessels of the merchant marine, known as the S Code in America.'[1]

Breaking Japan's Codes 133

The thing that we should come to understand is just how big a cover-up is still going on with the media and our government. The thing is, the American people are not stupid, when presented with the knowledge that a cover-up has taken place they will question why. The prime example of this is John F. Kennedy's assassination. The fact that over 94 per cent of Americans do not believe the official report anymore proves this point.

The next point to be made is the information known from these codes. It is now known that these codes were broken, so these intercepts were decoded in less than a day. However, the most damaging evidence has been destroyed, lost or is still considered Top Secret.

The one war message that was intercepted that told the Japanese Fleet to attack in Japanese is '*Niitaka Yama Nobore*, 1208' translated as 'Climb Mount Niitaka, 1208'. This message was intercepted on Hawaii on 2 December 1941 at 1.30 a.m. at Station H by Joseph Christie Howard. It was decoded by Howard, put into his log book and then sent through the intelligence pipeline. Anyone who was in intelligence knew that 'Climb Mount Niitaka' was the go-ahead message for Japanese planes to attack Pearl Harbor. This historical event has been covered up for seventy-nine years. The fact that Howard's message did not become public for fifty-eight years shows just how amazing the cover-up was, with these intercepts remaining locked up as top secret. Edwin Layton, an officer in Military Intelligence and an FDR stooge, would do his best to keep this top secret until he died in 1984. The true facts on this message will amaze any historian for the message 'Climb Mount Niitaka' was actually intercepted by three U.S. Navy listening posts: Corregidor, Guam, and Hawaii – and was ready to be sent to Admiral Hart and General MacArthur in Manila, and Admiral Kimmel and General Short in Hawaii and the U.S. Military Intelligence commanders in Washington D.C.. However, according to the official record none of these officials ever saw this message. A historian could believe that about Hart, MacArthur, Kimmel and Short but not the Military Intelligence officers in Washington D.C. The historian should remember Howard's message produced at least two official documents and to this day the United States Navy has censored Howard and this original paperwork. When Stinnett tried to get the documents released by the United States Navy, he was told in no certain terms that the answer was no.

The one last problem that should be addressed here is the Station VICTOR radio listening station on American Samoa that intercepted the message from a Japanese submarine that broke radio silence and showed that the Japanese fleet was heading in the direction of the Hawaiian Islands on the morning of 6 December 1941. This message was sent within an hour to the office of Joseph Rochefort (another FDR yes man) at HYPO on Pearl Harbor. If any historian decides to research these RDF fixes they will find over 300 pages missing from them of the many messages that originated with VICTOR during July through December 1941 because the United States Navy has them locked up in a vault at College Park, Maryland, and they are not to be viewed by the American public. This radio message from the Japanese submarine I-10 shows that the Japanese Navy was not keeping radio silence on its way to attack Pearl Harbor.

Below is a list of all messages intercepted and decoded by United States Military Intelligence from the Imperial Japanese Navy attack force for Hawaii before 7 December 1941:

    A. Radio transmissions by Admiral Nagumo: 60
    B. Tokyo radio to the vessels of the First Air Fleet: 24
    C. Broadcasts originated by Japanese carriers: 20
    D. Broadcasts originated by Carrier Division commanders: 12
    E. Messages originated by vessels attached to the First Air Fleet, but not carriers: 8
    F. Messages originated by the Midway Neutralization Unit: 4
    G. Tokyo radio to individual Carrier Division commanders: 1

This brings the number of intercepted radio messages to 129. The first intercepted message from Admiral Osami Nagano specified that Pearl

Harbor was to be attacked. To show that Admiral Kimmel knew of a probable attack by the Japanese on 7 December 1941, on 5 December he had Captain Charles H. McMorris draw up a secret action plan for the fleet if a war broke out with the Japanese and Hawaii was attacked within the next forty-eight hours. McMorris wrote up the action plan that kept all carriers out of Pearl Harbor: *Enterprise* and *Lexington* would be out on manoeuvres, while the *Saratoga* would be held on the coast of California. This action plan was approved by Kimmel on 5 December and sent to the commanders of each of these carriers. Again, one must remember that Kimmel was a FDR puppet, so again this order could have come from FDR with a foreknowledge of the attack, since he knew Yamamoto was after the carriers.

Chapter XI

Memos and Warnings to the Commanders at Pearl Harbor, 1941

The commanders at Pearl Harbor must share some of the blame for the attack for they were warned by Washington D.C. and the White House to be prepared and ready for an attack from the Imperial Japanese Navy. To start with below is a copy of a Hawaiian newspaper article printed seven days before the attack on Pearl Harbor that gives an uncanny prediction to what was to come one week later.

So any historian who wants to say FDR did not know the attack was coming on 7 December would need to explain this article. The problem is that they cannot, for it is there for anyone to read.

Another issue in the debate is the fact neither Admiral Kimmel nor General Short ever faced court martial. It is alleged this was to avoid disclosing information showing the U.S. had advanced knowledge of the attack. When asked, 'Will historians know more later?', Kimmel replied, 'I'll tell you what I believe. I think that most of the incriminating records have been destroyed. ... I doubt if the truth will ever emerge.' ...' From Vice Admiral Libby, 'I will go to my grave convinced that FDR ordered Pearl Harbor to let happen. He must have known.' It is equally likely this was done to avoid disclosing the fact that Japanese codes were being read, given that there was a war on. One key part of the controversy of the debate centers on the state of documents pertaining to the attack at Pearl Harbor on December 7th, 1941. There are many documents related to Pearl Harbor which have not yet been made public. Some may no longer exist, as many documents were destroyed early during the war due to fears of an impending Japanese invasion of Hawaii. Still others are partial and mutilated.

Information that is still currently classified includes key reports in Churchill's records, including the PREM 3 file in the UK's Public Records Office, which contains Churchill's most secret wartime intelligence briefs. In it, the 252 group dealing with the Japanese situation in 1941 is open, save for the omission of Section 5, dealing with events from November 1941 through March 1942, and is marked with official finality as 'closed for 75 years.' Unlike the Magic intelligence files released by the United States, none of the Ultra intelligence files pertaining to Japan have been released by the British government. Sheet No. 94644 derives from its reference in the FOIA-released Japanese Navy Movement Reports of Station H in November 1941. Entries for 28 November 1941 have several more items of interest, each being a 'movement code' message (indicating ship movements or movement orders), with specific details given by associated Sheet Numbers. Examples are: Sheet No. 94069 has information on 'KASUGA MARU' – this being hand-written (*Kasuga Maru* was later converted to CVE *Taiyo*); Sheet No. 94630 is associated with IJN oiler *Shiriya* (detailed to the Midway Neutralization Force, with destroyers *Ushio* and *Sazanami*, not the *Kido Butai*); and finally for Sheet No. 94644 there is another hand-written remark 'FAF using Akagi xtmr' (First Air Fleet using *Akagi*'s transmitter). It is known that the movement reports were largely readable at the time.

These three documents (Sheet Numbers 94069, 94630 and 94644) are examples of materials which yet, even after decades and numerous specific FOIA requests, have not been declassified fully and made available to the public. Sheet Number 94644, for example, noted as coming from *Akagi*'s transmitter and as being a 'movement code' report, would have likely contained a reported position.[2] The one thing that must also be considered when historians try and say that FDR never seen the McCollum Memo, is the fact that everything that was written in the McCollum memo was implemented by the United States, and the only person who could have had this done was President Franklin D. Roosevelt to start a war with Japan to get them to attack the United States. So when coming clean about the documents above, the United States needs to also come clean about the McCollum memo.

And with this information, the hits just keep on coming. Also the reader must understand that what they are reading here are facts, not a conspiracy theory that the media would want you to believe. Historians should even have a problem with the Pulitzer Prize that they give out for history, for they are doing a cover-up as well by not reporting the truth. The Pulitzer Prize needs to revamp itself and awarded the prize to actual historians and scholars of history.

The thing that the reader needs to understand is that the United States government has lied on numerous occasions when it comes to information on the attack on Pearl Harbor. The thing that should come to light for any historian is that on 16 November 1941 there was a huge monumental breakthrough by the CAST codebreakers for they had decoded the operational code of the Japanese Navy. This little titbit of information did not even come to be viewed by the American public until it was declassified from 'Top Secret' in May 2000. The other thing that should be remembered here is that at this time the Imperial Japanese Navy thought all of the 'Top Secret' messages it was sending were safe and secure. To state it simply, they were not, for America was intercepting them and decoding them. Japanese admirals sent out countless messages that made their plans crystal clear in the preceding weeks up until the attack on Pearl Harbor. These ONI messages that were intercepted and decoded were sent to FDR on a daily basis. The NSA and the Department of the United States Navy have kept from the American people over 133,000 intercepted messages from the Imperial Japanese Navy prior to the attack on Pearl Harbor in 1941. This does not include the American Navy files on the Imperial Japanese Navy that are also still 'Top Secret' today.

One only has to look at this private letter FDR sent to the Japanese Emperor to see that he was bullying Japan into a war. Although FDR already knew that the attack force was on its way to strike Pearl Harbor, this letter was a way to preserve his reputation.

II: MESSAGE FROM THE PRESIDENT TO THE EMPEROR OF JAPAN
(Dept. of State Bulletin, Vol. V, No. 129, Dec. 13, 1941)
The following message from the President to the Emperor of Japan was dispatched Saturday afternoon, December 6, and public announcement was made at that time that this message to the Emperor had been sent by the President:

Almost a century ago the President of the United States addressed to the Emperor of Japan a message extending an offer of friendship of the people of the United States to the people of Japan. That offer was accepted, and in the long period of unbroken peace and friendship which has followed, our respective nations, through the virtues of their peoples and the wisdom of their rulers have prospered and have substantially helped humanity.

Only in situations of extraordinary importance to our two countries need I address to Your Majesty messages on matters of state. I feel I should now so address you because of the deep and far-reaching emergency which appears to be in formation.

Developments are occurring in the Pacific area which threaten to deprive each of our nations and all humanity of the beneficial influence of the long peace between our two countries. Those developments contain tragic possibilities.

The people of the United States, believing in peace and in the right of nations to live and let live, have eagerly watched the conversations between our two Governments during these past months. We have hoped for a termination of the present conflict between Japan and China. We have hoped that a peace in the Pacific could be consummated in such a way that nationalities of many diverse peoples could exist side by side without fear of invasion; that unbearable burdens of armaments could be lifted for them all; and that all peoples would resume commerce without discrimination against or in favor of any nation.

I am certain that it will be clear to Your Majesty, as it is to me that in seeking these great objectives both Japan and the United States should agree to eliminate any form of military threat. This seemed essential to the attainment of the high objectives.

More than a year ago Your Majesty's Government concluded an agreement with the Vichy Government by which five or six thousand Japanese troops were permitted to enter into Northern French Indo-China for the protection of Japanese troops which were operating against China further north. And this Spring and Summer the Vichy Government permitted further Japanese military forces to enter into Southern French Indo-China for the common defense of French Indo-China. I think I am correct in saying that no attack has been made upon Indo-China, nor that any has been contemplated.

During the past few weeks it has become clear to the world that Japanese military, naval and air forces have been sent to Southern Indo-China in such large numbers as to create a reasonable doubt on the part of other nations that this continuing concentration in Indo-China is not defensive in its character.

Because these continuing concentrations in Indo-China have reached such large proportions and because they extend now to the southeast and the southwest corners of that Peninsula, it is only reasonable that the people of the Philippines, of the hundreds of Islands of the East Indies, of Malaya and of Thailand itself are asking themselves whether these forces of Japan are preparing or intending to make attack in one or more of these many directions.

I am sure that Your Majesty will understand that the fear of all these peoples is a legitimate fear inasmuch as it involves their peace and their national existence. I am sure that Your Majesty will understand why the people of the United States in such large numbers look askance at the establishment of military, naval and air bases manned and equipped so greatly as to constitute armed forces capable of measures of offense.

It is clear that a continuance of such a situation is unthinkable.

None of the peoples whom I have spoken of above can sit either indefinitely or permanently on a keg of dynamite.

There is absolutely no thought on the part of the United States of invading Indo-China if every Japanese soldier or sailor were to be withdrawn there from.

I think that we can obtain the same assurance from the Governments of the East Indies, the Governments of Malaya and the Government of Thailand. I would even undertake to ask for the same assurance on the part of the Government of China. Thus a withdrawal of the Japanese forces from Indo-China would result in the assurance of peace throughout the whole of the South Pacific area.

I address myself to Your Majesty at this moment in the fervent hope that Your Majesty may, as I am doing, give thought in this definite emergency to a way of dispelling the dark clouds. I am confident that both of us, for the sake of the peoples not only of our own great countries but for the sake of humanity in neighboring territories, have a sacred duty to restore traditional amity and prevent further death and destruction in the world.[3]

FDR had already put into action a plan to get the Japanese to attack the United States and the fact that he sent this message only proves the point that he already knew of the intention to attack Pearl Harbor on 7 December from all the intelligence information he had received since 1925 on Japan's intentions to take control of all the Pacific. This was just the final blow to ensure that Japan would attack Pearl Harbor. Again this is a form of treason when a commander-in-chief allows his men to be killed just to ensure that America would back him to get the United States into the war. One of the more compelling pieces of evidence used in support of the theory is a declassified memo dated 4 December 1941 that was released in 2017. In it Hawaii was noted as a 'Point of Attack' for the Japanese military. This message was sent to Washington D.C., so a historian must assume that something of this calibre would have been sent directly to FDR. The fact is FDR and his commanders knew in advance that Pearl Harbor was going to be attacked on 7 December.

The amazing thing that should persuade any historian that a cover-up is still going on today about the attack on Pearl Harbor is to try and get information from the CIA webpage and it will tell you that it is still classified as a matter of national security. The question that should be asked is why would it still be considered of this status since it has been eighty years since Pearl Harbor? The cover-up began way back in 1945 with an investigation into the attack.

Investigation
On August 28, 1945, President Truman issued an executive order directing several government departments and the joint chiefs of staff

'to take such steps as are necessary to prevent release to the public' information related to a U.S. cryptanalysis program to crack Japanese coded transmissions. When Congress formed the Pearl Harbor Committee a few weeks later, members objected to the withholding of information by the executive branch. The president revised the order, directing some individuals to 'make available to the Joint Committee on the Investigation of Pearl Harbor Attack ... any information in their possession material to the investigation.'

Though numerous investigations of the attack preceded the congressional inquiry, some files related to the attack had never been located. Partly to facilitate the search for missing documents and partly because, in the words of one historian, Republicans 'did not trust counsel to find and produce all relevant information,' Senator Owen Brewster proposed a resolution to authorize individual committee members 'in company with a member of the staff, to examine any records deemed to be relevant to the current investigation.' The committee voted down Brewster's resolution on a straight party-line vote. Senators Homer Ferguson and Brewster, both members of the Special Committee to Investigate the National Defense Program (also known as the Truman committee) were seasoned investigators. Frustrated by the committee's decision, they appealed to their colleagues from the Senate floor. Senator Brewster complained that committee members had not been 'granted the same latitude in the examination of governmental records that was always accorded without question during the history of the Truman committee.' The Pearl Harbor investigation, Brewster urged, should pursue new lines of inquiry, rather than 'review what had already been put in the record.' Senator Ferguson asked, 'Are we confined in our investigation only to the matters appearing in the existing official reports?' In reality, the executive branch deluged the committee with documents and exhibits, prompting Senator Brewster to lodge his 'regret and protest – at the first public committee hearing about the 'premature beginning of this inquiry' noting, 'it is just a physical impossibility to go over the [more than 1,000 exhibits] prior to this hearing.'

Disagreements over committee procedure led, at times, to acrimonious exchanges among senators on the Senate floor. James Tunnell of Delaware denounced Brewster and Ferguson's demands for greater access to material as a partisan plan to 'dig up something' that could be used to 'besmirch the reputation of the Nation's wartime Commander in Chief [Franklin Roosevelt].' Brewster dismissed Tunnell's 'extreme attack' as an inaccurate characterization of his effort to simply 'explore the files.'

Debates over procedure were driven, at least in part, by Republican concerns that Barkley's long-standing allegiance to President Roosevelt made him incapable of objectively pursuing the Pearl Harbor inquiry. Barkley's close association with the president dated to 1937 when Roosevelt intervened on Barkley's behalf to ensure his election as majority leader and continued until Roosevelt's death on April 12, 1945. As one historian observed, 'Barkley accepted his role of presidential flag carrier, but it took him years to regain confidence or to command the loyalty' of members of his own party.

Outcome
The eight members who signed the majority report found that 'officers, both in Washington and Hawaii, were fully conscious of the danger from air attack.' The Hawaiian commands and the Intelligence and War Plans Divisions of the War and Navy Departments made 'errors of judgment and not derelictions of duty.' Authors rejected the claim that President Roosevelt and top advisors 'tricked, provoked, incited, cajoled, or coerced Japan' into attacking the United States in order to draw the nation into war.

Senators Brewster and Ferguson penned a minority report, dismissing the majority's conclusions as 'illogical.' 'When all the testimony, papers, documents, exhibits, and other evidence duly laid

Memos and Warnings to the Commanders at Pearl Harbor, 1941

before the Committee are reviewed,' they wrote, 'it becomes apparent that the record is far from complete.'

In the end, the committee left many questions unanswered. 'Why, with some of the finest intelligence available in our history,' wondered the committee, 'why was it possible for a Pearl Harbor to occur?' The majority report recommended centralizing 'operational and intelligence work' and drawing more 'clear-cut' lines of responsibility among intelligence agencies. Some of these recommendations became law when Congress passed and the president signed the National Security Act of 1947. The law consolidated the military into a newly formed Department of Defense directed by a secretary of defense. The act also established the Central Intelligence Agency to gather and evaluate intelligence related to national security.[4] [The committee should have asked how and why did such a cover-up take place.]

Since the founding of the CIA, information has been classified under national security on many different levels. Information gets destroyed, disappears, and is locked up in vaults for eighty or more years to hide the truth from the American people.

The documents below should make every American's blood boil for these messages were intercepted from the Japanese Navy and decoded by the Office of Naval Intelligence (ONI) prior to the attack on Pearl Harbor telling exactly how the attack was going to take place. However, FDR ignored these highly important intercepts and the question must be asked, why? Since FDR had to know that the attack was coming, then why did he not alert these commanders? The next question that must be asked is was it a coincidence that Admiral Kimmel sent dispatches to each ship in his carrier force on Friday, 5 December 1941 to stay out at sea and not return until 8 December unless he was privy to this information and FDR told him to stand down to allow the attack to take place. Then, the question must be asked, why is this information just starting to come to light after eighty years?

25 November 1941
Appendix D
Selected Intelligence Documents, 1940-41
From: CinC Combined Fleet
To: First Air Fleet
(Pearl Harbor Attack Force)

The task force, keeping its movement strictly secret and maintaining close guard against submarines and aircraft, shall advance into Hawaiian waters, and upon the very opening of hostilities shall attack the main force of the United States Fleet in Hawaii and deal it a mortal blow. The first raid is planned for the dawn of X-Day (exact date to be given by later order).

Upon completion of the air raid, the task force, keeping close coordination and guarding against the enemy's counterattack, shall speedily leave the enemy waters and then return to Japan.

Should the negotiations with the United States prove successful, the task force shall hold itself in readiness forthwith to return and reassemble.[5]

This intercept is shattering to any historian who believes that FDR did not know when the attack on Pearl Harbor was coming. Even General Douglas MacArthur knew the attack was coming very soon, for he let FDR know that he would not go on the offensive but would set up a successful defence (this was probably due to the fact that FDR had not supplied him with the necessary equipment to go on the offensive, even to the point that he truly could not even mount a good defensive position.) This actually played directly into what FDR wanted to happen and that was for Japan to undertake the first overt act of war. (Again, Japan had already done this in 1937 with the sinking of the *Panay* on the Yangtze River.)

Declassified
Authority NND 770055
Cablegram
Received by War Department Message Center
Room 3441 Munitions Bldg., Washington D.C.
November 28th, 1941
453A-M
From: Manila, Philippines
To: General George C. Marshall
SECRET
NO. 1004 NOVEMBER TWENTY EIGHT
PURSUANT TO INSTRUCTIONS CONTAINED IN YOUR RADIO SIX TWO FOUR AIR RECONNAISSANCE HAS EXTENDED AND INTENSIFIED IN CONJUNCTION WITH THE NAVY STOP! GROUND SECURITY MEASURES HAVE BEEN TAKEN STOP! WITHIN THE LIMITATIONS IMPOSED BY PRESENT STATE OF DEVELOPMENT OF THIS THEATRE OF OPERATIONS EVERYTHING IS IN READINESS FOR THE CONDUCT OF A SUCCESSFUL DEFENSE STOP! INTIMATE LIAISON AND COOPERATION AND CORDIAL RELATIONS EXIST BETWEEN ARMY AND NAVY.

MacArthur
36 A G O
December 3rd, 1941
Received
SECRET[6]

The message below to General Marshall from General MacArthur demonstrates that FDR knew the attack was coming in Hawaii and the Philippines. It is is suggested that FDR and his command staff in

Washington D.C wanted the American public to believe that they were surprise attacks by the Imperial Japanese.

This next messages were sent out to the Army and Navy commanders Admiral Kimmel and Lt General Short on the seriousness of the situation with Imperial Japan. However, if a historian looks closely at these messages, which were sent out by Admiral Stark and General Marshall of FDR's Washington staff, it looks more like they were just covering themselves so that when the attack came they, along with the President, would not be held to blame. The same message was sent out by both Stark and Marshall, with this one sent to Kimmel.

> From: Chief of Naval Operations
> Released By: Admiral H. Stark COM-PNITCF
> Date: November 28th, 1941 COM-PSNCF
> REFER TO MY 272338 X ARMY HAS SENT FOLLOWING TO COMMANDER WESTERN DEFENSE COMMAND QUOTE NEGOTIATIONS WITH JAPAN APPEAR TO BE TERMINATED TO ALL PRACTICAL PURPOSES WITH ONLY THE BAREST POSSIBILITIES THAT THE JAPANESE GOVERNMENT MIGHT COME BACK AND OFFER TO CONTINUE X JAPANESE FUTURE ACTION UNPREDICTABLE BUT HOSTILE ACTION POSSIBLE AT ANY MOMENT X IF HOSTILITIES CANNOT REPEAT NOT BE AVOIDED THE UNITED STATES DESIRES THAT JAPAN COMMITS THE FIRST OVERT ACT X THIS POLICY SHOULD NOT REPEAT NOT BE CONSTRUED AS RESTRICTING YOU TO A COURSE OF ACTION THAT MIGHT JEOPARDIZE YOUR DEFENSE X PRIOR TO HOSTILE JAPANESE ACTION YOU ARE DIRECTED TO UNDERTAKE SUCH RECONNAISSANCE AND OTHER MEASURES AS YOU DEEM NECESSARY BUT THESE MEASURES

Memos and Warnings to the Commanders at Pearl Harbor, 1941

SHOULD BE CARRIED OUT SO AS NOT REPEAT NOT TO ALARM CIVIL POPULATION OR DUSCLOSE INTENT X REPORT MEASURES TAKEN X A SEPARATE MESSAGE IS BEING SENT TO ARMY NINTH CORPS. TOP SECRET
Make original copy only; deliver to communications Watch Officer in person.[7]

This message from Admiral Stark and General Marshall is so important in understanding that FDR knew when the attack was coming, for it contains the simple statement: 'If hostilities cannot repeat cannot be avoided, the United States desires that Japan commit the first overt act.' There is no way a historian can avoid that this message states FDR knew the attack on Hawaii and Pearl Harbor was coming. Not only that but Admiral Stark and General Marshall were acting on FDR's orders, to follow the United States Government agenda and allow Japan to make the first overt act of war. This should really make any historian truly consider the statement General George Marshall made to his command staff, 'Gentlemen, we must take what we know about Pearl Harbor with us to our grave.'

Another thing that historians who defend FDR always avoid is that the following message was intercepted and decoded on 2 December 1941. Naval Intelligence knew what the message ordered; an attack on Pearl Harbor, for to climb Mount Niitaka is a great feat, as would be the destruction of the American Navy at Pearl Harbor.

2 Dec
From: CINC-Combined
To: Combined Flt
'This dispatch is top secret. This order is effective at 1730 on 2 December. Climb Mount Niitaka 1208, repeat 1208.'
TOP SECRET ULTRA[8]

Historians and scholars must remember that this message was intercepted five days before the attack on Pearl Harbor took place. It was sent to Washington D.C. and yet no action was taken, despite FDR knowing its meaning. Below are excerpts from the U.S. Navy Cryptologic Series on Pearl Harbor from the months prior to the attack. This information was not released until 1993:

> Army and Navy Sites Authorized to Intercept Diplomatic Traffic, August 1940
> Army Navy Site location Site designator Number of collectors
> Site location
> Site designator Number of Collectors
> Fort Monmouth, NJ 1 19 Winter Harbor, ME W 8 Presidio, CA 2 9 Amagansett, NY G 4 Fort Sam Houston, TX 3 14 Cheltenham, MD M 20 Corozal, CZ [Panama Canal Zone] 4 20 Jupiter, FL J 4 Fort Shafter, HI 5 19 Bainbridge Island, WA S 12 Fort Hunt, VA 724 Heeia, HI H 8
> Totals 6 105 6 56[9]

Any historian writing about the truth of the attack on Pearl Harbor and the Philippines can see by the number of intercept radio stations in operation in 1941 that they could crack the codes of the Japanese and intercept them to send to Washington D.C. to keep FDR appraised as to what was taking place from day to day. It is truly inconceivable to believe that FDR did not know the attack date.

On 25 November 1941 Japan's Admiral Yamamoto sent a radio message to the group of Japanese warships that would attack Pearl Harbor. Newly released naval records prove that from 17 to 25 November the United States Navy intercepted eighty-three messages that Yamamoto sent to his carriers. Part of the 25 November message reads: 'the task force, keeping its movements strictly secret and maintaining close guard against submarines and aircraft, shall advance into Hawaiian waters, and upon the very opening of hostilities shall attack the main force of the United States fleet in Hawaii and deal it a mortal blow ...'[10] This message was intercepted and sent to FDR. The problem that should be addressed to politicians, both Republican and Democrat, is why are there still thousands of documents still classified as 'Top Secret', or the documents that have been released have been censored so that no one can read them? This does not even include the 133,000 intercept messages of the Japanese that have been either locked away or destroyed by the U.S. Navy. It is truly amazing how today the only thing politicians care about is their own agenda instead of looking out for the American people.

When you consider the sheer weight of circumstantial evidence – the specific warnings about the attack, the pro-war political imperative of Roosevelt, and the planning that went into the imminent war against the Axis – it seems far more likely than not that the US allowed the attack on Pearl Harbor to take place. However, it is just not the circumstantial evidence that shows this. There are the documented facts that historians cannot ignore anymore. The problem is that historians and scholars are not the ones writing history now. Journalists who know nothing of history and fail to undertake proper research are writing books that only care about a politically correct history, instead of writing about the truth of a historical event. So instead of getting a true history in the media, the American public gets a false one.

Until historians, scholars and journalists stand up and say enough is enough, this false history will not stop, and in letting it continue our children are not learning what they should be learning about history in school. The attack on Pearl Harbor is an excellent example. The fact that all of these documents have not been released after eighty years testifies to this fact. Then also remember that FDR also had thousands of documents destroyed right after the attack on Pearl Harbor using the ruse that it was to prevent them falling into Japanese hands. The real reason is that FDR was covering his action by destroying the evidence.

Chapter XII

Attack on Pearl Harbor, 1941

The attack on Pearl Harbor did not start from the air, but from under the ocean with the mini attack submarines of the Imperial Japanese Navy. Historians and scholars should ask why Admiral Kimmel did not set up submarine and torpedo mesh nets to keep these mini-submarines out and also reduce the effectiveness of Japanese torpedo bombers. This could have been very effective in protecting the fleet in Pearl Harbor. A historian must ask the question, 'Why did Kimmel not put out the nets?' The fact that there were no nets put in place puts Kimmel in the hot seat, unless FDR had ordered him not to. This is a question that will never be answered.

Even though these midget submarines did very little in the attack on Pearl Harbor, the sinking of one should have brought every soldier and sailor to an alert stand-to; why it did not may never truly be answered. (The commanders were already on alert status of possible attack.) The sinking and spotting of this sub was a good three and half hours before the Japanese planes got to Pearl Harbor. The message was sent that a sub had been sunk and no ship in the harbor was even warned of this incident. If action had been taken U.S. fighter planes could have been in the air to meet the Japanese attack force and ships could have been out of the harbor waiting for the attack to come. It does not take a rocket scientist to understand how this could have changed the outcome to the attack on Pearl Harbor.

The attack on Pearl Harbor marked the official entry of the U.S. into the war.

It is very important for Americans to know these heroes that were at Pearl Harbor that day. We should never forget these young men.

Attack on Pearl Harbor, 1941

Pearl Harbor! On December 7, 1941 Japanese forces attacked United States naval and air bases in the Hawaiian Islands, and scored a major victory. Over 2,300 U.S. military personnel lost their lives – almost half of them crew of the battleship Arizona which was blown up and sunk in the harbor by bombs and torpedoes – and the U. S. Pacific fleet was devastated. The next day President Franklin Roosevelt called for a declaration of war, and described the Japanese attack as 'a date which will live in infamy.' [Over the years many Americans have disagreed with that judgment. And they asked the question, 'What did FDR know prior to the attack?]

Just why was Pearl Harbor 'infamous'? The Japanese planes attacked strictly military targets and there were relatively few civilian casualties. The battle was a terrible defeat for the American armed forces, which were taken completely by surprise. But a surprise attack is not infamous in wartime; every military commander would attack by surprise if possible. Nor did the bitter facts of U.S. defeat and heavy losses make the raid criminal. There is just one reason the operation was infamous: because it was an act of military aggression. Japan and the United States were not then at war, although their conflicting interests were threatening to turn violent. The attack turned a dispute into a war; Pearl Harbor was a crime because the Japanese struck first.

That is exactly what Japan did in 1941. There is no question that the United States posed a huge threat to what Japanese leaders considered to be vital national interests. The U.S. Navy, in particular, was potentially a major obstacle to Japanese expansion in China and Southeast Asia. Moreover, the United States had imposed an embargo on oil and steel shipments to Japan, a nation that depended on imports and had oil reserves sufficient for only about two years.[1]

However, this is no defense, there is no such thing as a pre-emptive strike. To attack for economic reasons is not a defense for any country to use, and it must also be remembered that Japan had already put its plan into effect in 1927 with the Tanaka Memorial. So another thing any historian should remember is that this document in the hands of Japan would have been damaging to their defense in court, so like thousands of other documents that were destroyed by Japan before the end of the war to hide their guilt, any historian should realize this about this document. One only has to look at the documents that they destroyed about the murdering and treatment of Allied PoWs and an excellent example of this was the Palawan massacre. The only way America found out about it was because a few PoWs escaped from it. The Imperial Japanese Government ordered all documents pertaining to Allied prisoners of war be destroyed.

Below are two different ship deck logs of the morning of the attack on Pearl Harbor. These logs showed what these young men had to endure and go through on 7 December 1941 and what those who survived would have to live with for the rest of their lives. The first deck log is from the USS *Maryland*, which describes what took place on that ship that day during the early morning hours.

The second deck log is from the USS *Dale* and it too describes what was taking place on that ship during the early morning hours of 7 December. Unlike FDR and his staff in Washington, they were not privy to the information that the Imperial Japanese Navy was going to attack Pearl Harbor on this date. These sailors were just going about their everyday duties when the attack occurred. These young men were set up as sacrificial lambs to the slaughter by President Franklin D. Roosevelt and his command staff in Washington D.C. to get America into a war with Japan that should have already started in 1937 with the sinking of the *Panay*.

Attack on Pearl Harbor, 1941

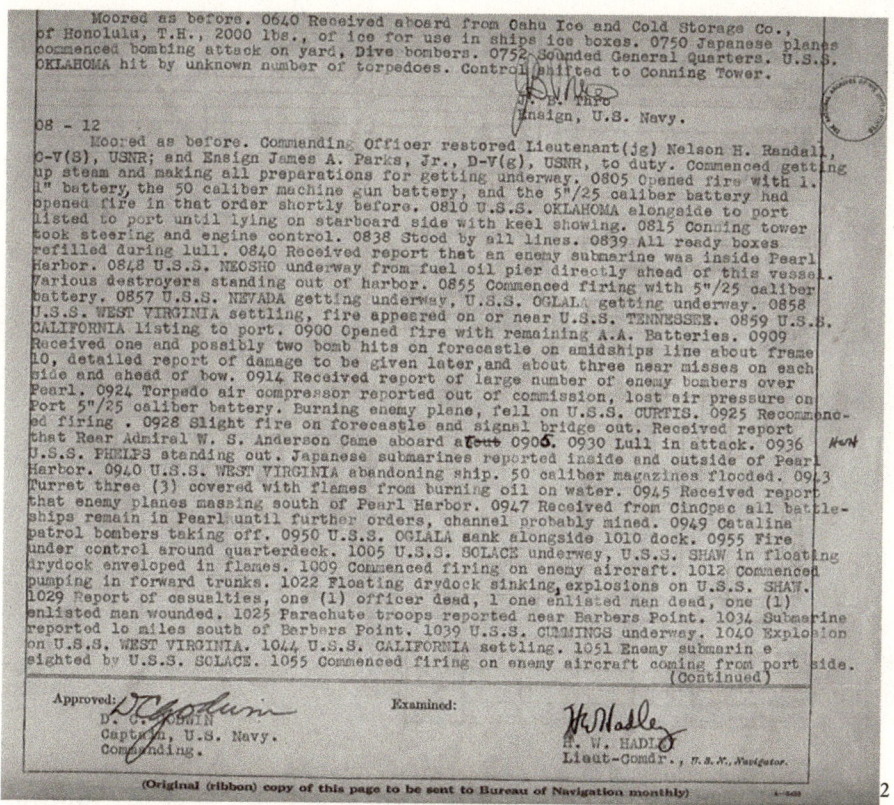

Many of these young sailors aboard would lose their lives when the attack by the Japanese Navy commenced. It will never be known how many of the men would have survived if they had known the attack was coming. The question that should be asked, 'Is why was this allowed to happen?'

```
04-08
     Moored as before.  0758 Waves of torpedo planes, level bombers, and dive
bombers marked with Japanese insigna attacked Pearl Harbor; Sounded general
quarters set condition afirm lit off boilers #1 and #2 and #4.  Breaking out
ammunition.
                                        F.M. RADEL
                                        Ensign, U.S. Navy

08-12
     Moored as before.  0810 Opened fire on planes with machine guns followed
by main battery.  0815 One enemy plane believed shot down by machine gun
fire from USS DALE.  0825 Boilers #1,#2 and #4 cut in on main line.  0836
Underway on various courses and at various speeds proceeding out of Pearl
Harbor. Ensign F.M. RADEL,U.S.N. Commanding Officer, following named Officers
and men absent:- Lt.Comdr. A.L.Rorschach,U.S.N.   Lt. R.L. Moore, Jr. U.S.N.
Ensign K.G. Robinson, U.S.N.  Ensign D.J. Vellis U.S.N.  Ensign L.C. Huntley,
U.S.N.R.  Ensign M.D. Callahan U.S.N.R.   EDWARDS, G.L. CMM U.S.N. WARREN,
R.H. F.C.1c U.S.N.  COULSON, S. E.M. 2c, U.S.N. SMITH,J.V. Sea 1c, U.S.N.
FALCONER, D.D. Y1c, U.S.N. NEHRING, R.A. F.C. 3c, U.S.N. GAMBILL, M. M.M.1c,
U.S.N.  ENGLISH, J.P. M.M. 1c,U.S.N.  JENNINGS, A.V. F.2c, U.S.N. 0844
Stopped while USS MONAGHAN dropped two depth charges on what was thought
to be and enemy submarine near USS CURTISS.  0848 Changed speed to 25 knots
proceeding out of channel. 0907 Passed Pearl Harbor entrance buoy #1 passed
from Inland to International waters. 0909 Established off shore patrol in
sector #1 on various courses and at various speeds maneuvering to avoid
strafing and bombing attacks.  0911 Shot down enemy dive bomber with .50
Caliber machine gun fire.  0959 Investigated small boat carrying small white
flag with several Oriental passengers. 1114 Joined up with USS WORDEN (CDS-1)
on course 340°T, 328°psc, speed 11 knots.  1149 Formed column, order of ships
in column WORDEN, AYLWIN, DALE and FARRAGUT: on course 271°T, 260°psc, speed
25 knots.
                                        F.M. RADEL
                                        Ensign, U.S. Navy
```

The blame for this attack has been laid at the feet of Admiral Kimmel and Lt General Short. The historian should understand that, yes, they do bear some of the responsibility but the main culprit is FDR and his staff in Washington D.C.. Historians and scholars report that when FDR's staff heard about the attack, they were shocked, but this was not from not knowing but because of how successful it had been. The simple fact is that the commanders in Washington D.C. knew of the attack before it took place.

At 6:00 a.m. on December 7 the Japanese fleet was 230 miles north of Oahu. Six carriers turned into the wind and launched the first wave – 183 planes. At the launching, two Zero fighters dropped from the mission: One crashed into the sea on takeoff, another developed engine trouble and was left on board the carrier. At 6:20 Commander Fuchida led the first wave of planes toward Pearl Harbor.

As soon as the first wave departed, the carrier crews readied the second wave. At 7:05 the carriers again swung eastward into the wind and began launching 167 aircraft. As before, the first lift-offs were the Nakajima B5 N2 'Kates,' which served as torpedo bombers on the first wave, and as horizontal bombers on the first and second waves. The Kates were followed by the Aichi D3A1 'Vals' (dive bombers) and Mitsubishi A6M2 Reisen Zero fighters. Only one dive bomber from the HIRYU developed engine trouble and failed to make the trip, leaving 350 planes in the air.

Meanwhile on Oahu, two warnings of the impending attack occurred. In the waters just outside the entrance to Pearl Harbor, the destroyer WARD at 6:30 a.m. fired on, depth-charged and sank a submarine within the defensive sea area. Bureaucratic delays and the need for confirmation caused an hour to go by before the report was forwarded to Admiral Husband E. Kimmel, commander in chief of the U.S. Pacific Fleet.

The second warning occurred at 7:02 a.m., nearly half an hour after the WARD fired the first shot of America's Pacific War. Two Army radar operators at the Opana station above Kahuku Point on Oahu's north shore picked up a large formation of planes on their radar screens. After checking and rechecking equipment, they notified the watch officer at Fort Shafter. No action was taken because the officer believed the planes to be a flight of B-17s flying in from California.

Flying through thick cloud cover, Commander Fuchida thought for a moment he had overflown Oahu, but a sudden parting of the clouds revealed the island's north shore. The signal was given to assume attack formation. As Fuchida looked toward Pearl Harbor and the surrounding airfields, he was relieved to see that the attack was a surprise, and the earlier report of Kido Butai's scout plane 'Enemy fleet in port!' was accurate. To Fuchida's disappointment, the prime targets of the attack – the aircraft carriers – were absent. Changing their plan, the torpedo planes concentrated on the battleships lined up along Battleship Row and the east side of Ford Island.

With assignments memorized by constant training, the first wave of planes attacked at 7:55 a.m. At about the same time, fighters and dive bombers hit the airfields at Kaneohe, Hickam, Ewa, Bellows and Wheeler. Within two hours, most American air power in Hawaii was destroyed.

At Pearl Harbor, as morning colors were readied and sailors and civilians ate breakfast, the Japanese planes struck. In 15 minutes the main battle line of the Pacific fleet was neutralized. The battleships CALIFORNIA, OKLAHOMA, WEST VIRGINIA, NEVADA and ARIZONA were sunk, as was the old battleship UTAH then being used as a target and anti-aircraft training vessel. The battleships MARYLAND, TENNESSEE and PENNSYLVANIA were damaged. Initially, the American response to the attack was sporadic, but within five minutes American vessels began to fire back in earnest against the attackers. 'Air Raid Pearl Harbor, this is no drill!' was relayed to the fleet.

The assault of the first wave ended about 8:45 a.m. There was a momentary lull before the second wave of Japanese planes arrived at 8:50 a.m. No torpedo planes came with the second group of dive and high-altitude bombers.

As the second wave withdrew, Fuchida circled Pearl Harbor and assessed the damage. Satisfied, he took a last look and signaled his pilots to return to the carrier. The main objective of the attack – demobilizing the Pacific Fleet – had been accomplished. More than 2,400 Americans were killed and 1,104 wounded. Twenty-one ships of the Pacific Fleet had been sunk or damaged, and 75 percent of the planes on the airfields surrounding Pearl Harbor were damaged or destroyed.

It was nearly 10 o'clock when the first wave of Japanese aircraft began landing on their carriers. By noon, the last planes had been recovered. Twenty-nine Japanese planes were lost, along with 55 airmen. The Special Attack Unit of midget submarines had lost 10 crewmen and all five boats, one boat and one prisoner were captured by Americans the following day on the beaches near Bellows Airfield.

Fuchida was gratified to see planes being readied for a third assault because many targets had been left untouched, particularly the naval shipyard, oil-storage facilities, and a number of American ships. While he wondered when the third wave would be launched, a heated debate was under way on the bridge of the fleet flagship HIJMS AKAGI.

Admiral Nagumo had feared the operation would not be successful, yet he had achieved successful results with minimal casualties. It was his contention that the mission was accomplished. Furthermore, the fleet's fuel was running low. More important, American carriers and other ships not in port were now searching for him. At 1 o'clock the task force altered course and began its journey back to Japan. This decision was a major blunder that greatly minimized the long-term effects of the attack on the American war machine.[4]

This next small section is a photo montage of what took place on 7 December at the Pearl Harbor Naval Base.

These images of the attack by the Imperial Japanese Navy at Pearl Harbor should never be forgotten, for to forget would allow another imperialist country to plan and attack again somewhere else in the world.

Gunner's mate Paul Aschbrenner was a 19-year-old sailor from Sumner who had joined the Navy the year before because there were no jobs available near his home. He had been assigned to the battleship USS *Oklahoma*, which was docked in Pearl Harbor. The attack began at 7.55 a.m. Hawaiian time. After the first torpedoes struck the *Oklahoma*, the lights went out and Aschbrenner found himself deep inside the ship in the dark.

The dive bombing and torpedo attacks lasted for a little more than an hour. For Aschbrenner and everyone else at Pearl Harbor, the attack had been a complete surprise. As the Japanese planes flew away, 2,500 American soldiers, sailors, and marines were either dead or missing.

The view of Commander Fushida on the air attack on Pearl Harbor is given here in a transcript of court proceedings:

> In September, 1941, I was transferred from the staff of the Third Carrier Division to aircraft carrier *Akagi*, a position I had left just one year earlier. Shortly after joining my old comrades in *Akagi*, I was given additional duty as commander of all air groups of the First Air Fleet. This was an assignment beyond all my dreams. I felt that something big must be afoot.
>
> It was at Kagoshima on the southern tip of Kyushu that I first learned the magnitude of events in store for me. My good friend Commander Genda, air operations officer on the staff of the First Air Fleet, came to see me at the air base and said, 'Now don't be alarmed, Fuchida, but we want you to lead our air force in the event that we attack Pearl Harbor!'
>
> Don't be alarmed? It was all I could do to catch my breath, and almost before I had done so we were on our way out to board *Akagi*, then anchored in Ariake Bay, for a conference with First Air Fleet commander, Vice Admiral Chuichi Nagumo, and his staff, including Chief of Staff, Rear Admiral Ryunosuke Kusaka.
>
> The more I heard about the plan the more astonishing it seemed. Genda kept urging that torpedoes be used against ships in Pearl Harbor; a feat that seemed next to impossible in view of

the water depth of only twelve meters, and the harbor being not more than five hundred meters in width. When I pointed this out, Genda merely grew more aggressive, insisting that if we could launch torpedoes, they would not be expected, it would add to the surprise of the attack and multiply their effectiveness. This line of argument won me over, and, despite the technical difficulties that would have to be overcome, I agreed to include torpedoes in our attack plans.

Shallow-water torpedo launching was not the only difficult problem I had to cope with. From ordinary fleet practice we had to shift our energies to specific training for this all-important mission calling for vast and intensive preparations; and, what is more, everything had to be done in haste. It was already late September, and the attack plan called for execution in December!

There was no time to lose. Our fliers had to work at the hardest kind of training. An added handicap to our efforts lay in the fact that, for security reasons, the pilots could not be told about the plans. Our progress was slow, especially with the problem of launching torpedoes in shallow water. Against my will I had to demand more and more of every man, yet none complained. They seemed to sense the intensification of the international situation and gave of themselves unquestioningly.

It was not until early November that the torpedo problem was finally solved by fixing additional fins to the torpedoes, and then my greatest worry was over. I was indeed proud of my men and felt honored to be their commander and participate in this great attack.

In mid-November First Air Fleet planes were taken on board their respective carriers, which then headed for the Kuriles, traveling singly and taking separate courses to avoid attention. By the 22nd the entire force had assembled in isolated Tankan Bay on Etorofu, second island from the southern end of the chain extending northeast from Hokkaido. This force consisted of carriers *Akagi, Kaga, Soryu, Hiryu, Shokaku, Zuikaku*, battleships *Hiei, Kirishima*; heavy cruisers *Tone*, *Chikuma*; light cruiser *Abukuma*; destroyers *Urakaze*, *Isokaze*, *Tanikaze*, *Hamakaze*, *Kazumi*, *Arare*, *Kagero*, *Shiranuhi*, *Akigumo*; submarines 1-19, 1-21, 1-23; and tankers *Kyokuto Maru*, *Kenyo Maru*, *Kokuyo Maru*, *Shinkoku Maru*, *Akebono Maru*, *Toho Maru*, *Toei Maru*, and *Nihon Maru*.

The following order was issued from Tokyo on the day that *Akagi* sailed into Tankan Bay:

Imperial General Headquarters
Navy Order No.5
21 November 1941
To: Commander in Chief Combined Fleet Isoroku Yamamoto
Via: Chief of Naval General Staff Osami Nagano By Imperial Order
1. Commander in Chief Combined Fleet will, at an appropriate time, dispatch to stand-by points necessary forces for execution of operations.
2. Commander in Chief Combined Fleet is empowered to use force in self defense in case his fleet is challenged by American, British or Dutch forces during the process of carrying out military preparations.
3. Detailed instructions will be given by the Chief of the Naval General Staff.

Four days later Admiral Yamamoto accordingly issued an operation order from his flagship *Nagato* at Hiroshima to Vice Admiral Nagumo, in command of the Pearl Harbor Attack Force:

The Task Force will leave Tankan Bay on 26 November and, making every effort to conceal its movement, advance to the stand-by point, where fueling will be quickly completed.

The designated stand-by point was 42°N 170°W, over a thousand miles to the north of the Hawaiian Island chain.

At 0600 on the dark and cloudy morning of 26 November our 28-ship task force weighed anchor and sailed out into the waters of the North Pacific Ocean. The sortie was cloaked in complete secrecy. A patrol boat guarding the bay entrance flashed a message, 'Good luck on your mission.' But even that boat was unaware of our assignment. *Akagi* signaled, 'Thanks,' and passed by, her ensign fluttering in the morning breeze. It would not be long before this ensign was replaced by a combat flag.

But this did not mean that the arrow had already gone from the bow. 'In case negotiations with the U. S. reach a successful conclusion,' Nagumo had been instructed, 'the task force will put about immediately and return to the homeland.' Unaware of this, however, the crews shouted 'Banzai!' as they took what might be their last look at Japan.

On *Akagi*'s bridge Commander Gishiro Miura, the navigation officer, was concentrating all his energies on control of the ship. Whether we reached the scheduled launching point successfully rested entirely upon his shoulders. So tense was his appearance that it made us feel he was a completely different man. His usual jovial attitude had disappeared. He now wore shoes instead of his usual slippers, and he was neatly dressed, a decided change from his customary dirty, worn-out uniform. Captain Hasegawa, the skipper of the ship, stood beside him. Sitting at the flight desk control post under the bridge, I watched the gradually receding mountains of the Kuriles.

Young boys of the flying crews were boiling over with fighting spirit. Hard nights and days of training had been followed by hasty preparations, and now the sortie, which meant that they were going to war.

I felt their keen enthusiasm and was reassured. Still I could not help doubting whether Japan had the proper confidence for carrying out a war. At the same time, however, I fully realized my duty as a warrior to fight and win victory for my country.

Personally I was opposed to the operational policy. The idea of an attack on Pearl harbor was a good one, but I thought the plan should have called for complete destruction of the United States Pacific Fleet at the outset, followed by an invasion of the Hawaiian Islands to push America entirely out of the Central Pacific. The plan covered expansion to the south – the Philippines, Malaya, Hong Kong, Guam, and other such vulnerable positions. It was my opinion that if Pacific operations to the east proved successful, there would be no need for military operations in the south.

Since the United States was the main foe, I could not understand why operations were not aimed directly toward the east. Admiral Yamamoto was quoted as having said that he had no confidence in the outcome of war after the first year. Why then, did he not press and press the enemy in the first year to force an early conclusion to the war? Anyway, the immediate mission was to strike a telling blow, and my assignment carried a grave responsibility. At the time I thought, 'Who could be luckier than I?'

My thoughts continued: What if the Fleet is not in Pearl Harbor? In such a case we would seek out the enemy en route to the attack. If we should meet the enemy tomorrow would Nagumo withdraw? No, we should attack and destroy him, I thought, and if the Admiral showed any hesitation, I would volunteer my views on these matters.

Such thoughts came one after another, but one remained uppermost. I was determined to do my utmost for victory.

In the meantime, the fleet had assumed formation. The carriers sailed in parallel columns of three followed by the tankers. On the outside two battleships and two heavy cruisers took positions, the whole group encircled by a screen of the light cruiser and destroyers. The submarines patrolled about 200 miles ahead of our force. The course was direct to the stand-by point, speed was fourteen knots. The first fueling at sea was carried out five days after our sortie, on 30 November.

Since our departure from Tankan Bay, a strict alert had been kept against U. S. submarines. [The Japanese Navy did not need to worry about U.S. subs, for they were standing down.]

Our course was chosen to pass between the Aleutians and Midway Island so as to keep out of range of air patrols, some of which were supposed to extend 600 miles. Another concern during the cruise was how to avoid a chance meeting with foreign merchant ships. The three submarines sent ahead of the fleet were to report any ships sighted to the fleet, which would then alter course to avoid them.

If an enemy fleet was sighted before X-2 day, our force was to reverse course immediately and abandon the operation. On the other hand, if it was one day before X day, whether to reverse course or launch the attack was left to the discretion of the task force commander.

Meanwhile, deceptive measures were being taken elsewhere to cover up our movements. On 5, 6, and 7 December sailors of the Yokosuka Naval Barracks were sent to Tokyo on a sightseeing tour. In early December *Tatsuta Maru* of the N.Y.K. Line had even left Yokohama heading for Honolulu, and she reversed course only upon receipt of the news that hostilities had begun.

Since leaving Tankan Bay we had maintained our eastward course in complete secrecy, thanks to thick, low-hanging clouds. Moreover, on 30 November, 6 and 7 December, the sea, which we feared might be rough, was calm enough for easy fueling. The not-too-rough sea also made it easy to maintain and prepare planes, and gave the men, especially the flying crews, a much needed chance to relax.

The fleet observed strict radio silence, but concentrated on listening for broadcasts from Tokyo or Honolulu. Our predominant concern was to catch any word about the outbreak of war.

In Tokyo a liaison conference between the Government and the High Command was held every day from 27 to 30 November to discuss the U. S. proposal of the 26th. It was concluded that the proposal was an ultimatum tending to subjugate Japan and making war inevitable. At the liaison conference of the 30th the decision was made to go, to war. This conference also concluded that a message declaring the end of negotiations be sent to the U. S., but that efforts be continued to the last moment. The final decision for war was made at an Imperial Conference on 1 December.

Next day the General Staff issued the long-awaited order and our task force received the Combined Fleet dispatch of 1730 which said, 'X Day will be 8 December.'

Now the die was cast and our duty was clear. The fleet drove headlong to the east.

Why was 8 December chosen as X day? That was 7 December and Sunday, a day of rest, in Hawaii. Was this merely a bright idea to hit the U. S. Fleet off duty? No, it was not so simple as that. This day for the opening of hostilities had been coordinated with the time of the Malayan operations, where air raids and landings were scheduled for dawn. Favorable moonlight was a major consideration, three or four days after the full moon being the most desirable time, and on 8 December the moon was 19 days old.

There was another reason for choosing 8 December. Our information indicated that the fleet returned to harbor on weekends after training periods at sea, so there was great likelihood that it would be in Pearl Harbor on Sunday morning. All things considered, 8 December was the logical day for the attack.

Long before the planning of the Pearl Harbor attack we had been interested in fleet activities in the Hawaiian area. Our information showed:

1. The fleet either went out on Tuesday and returned on Friday, or went out on Friday and returned on Saturday of the next week. In either case, it stayed in harbor about a week. When it went out for two weeks, it would usually return by Sunday.
2. The fleet trained to the southeast of Pearl Harbor. Intercepted radio messages from planes flying between this training area and Pearl Harbor showed that these planes were in flight for forty to sixty minutes. Accordingly, the training area was estimated to be near Maui, and probably north of 19°N latitude.
3. It was hard to determine whether the fleet put in to any other port during training periods, and if so, where. There were some indications that it might go to Ludhiana or Malaya for a short while.

After Japan's decision to go to war had been sent to the Attack Force, intelligence reports on U. S. Fleet activities continued to be relayed to us from Tokyo. [Messages were still being sent to the fleet from Tokyo and the USA was intercepting them.]

The information was thorough, but the news was often delayed two or three days in reaching Tokyo. These reports from Imperial General Staff were generally as follows:

Issued 2200, 2 December; received 0017, 3 December
Activities in Pearl Harbor as of 0800/28 November:
Departed: 2 BB (*Oklahoma* and *Nevada*), 1 CV (*Enterprise*), 2 CA, 12 DD.
Arrived: 5 BB, 3 CA, 3 CL, 12 DD, 1 tanker.

Ships making port today are those which departed 22 November.

Ships in port on afternoon of 28 November estimated as follows:

6 BB (2 *Maryland* class, 2 *California* class, 2 *Pennsylvania* class)

1 CV (*Lexington*)

9 CA (5 *San Francisco* class, 3 *Chicago* class, and *Salt Lake City*)

5 CL (4 *Honolulu* class and *Omaha*)

Issued 2300, 3 December; received 0035, 4 December

Ships present Pearl Harbor on afternoon of 29 November:

District A (between Naval Yard and Ford Island)

KT (docks northwest of Naval Yard): *Pennsylvania* and *Arizona*

FV (mooring pillars): *California, Tennessee, Maryland,* and *West Virginia*

KS (naval yard repair dock): *Portland*

In docks: 2 CA, 1 DD

Elsewhere: 4 SS, 1 DD tender, 2 patrol ships, 2 tankers, 2 repair ships, 1 minesweeper

District B (sea area northwest of Ford Island)

FV (mooring pillars): *Lexington*

Elsewhere: *Utah*, 1 CA (*San Francisco* class), 2 CL (*Omaha* class), 3 gunboats

District C (East Loch)

3 CA, 2 CL (*Honolulu* class), 17 DD, 2 DD tenders

District D (Middle Loch)

12 minesweepers

District E (West Loch)

No ships

No changes observed by afternoon of 2 December. So far they do not seem to have been alerted. Shore leaves as usual.

Issued 2030, 4 December; received 0420, 5 December
So far no indications of sea patrol flights being conducted. It seems that occasional patrols are being made to Palmyra, Johnston and Midway Islands. Pearl Harbor patrols unknown.

Issued 2200, 6 December; received 1036, 7 December
Activities in Pearl Harbor on the morning of 5 December:
Arrived: *Oklahoma* and *Nevada* (having been out for eight days)
Departed: *Lexington* and five heavy cruisers
Ships in harbor as of 1800, 5 December:
8 BB, 3 CL, 16 DD
In docks: 4 CL (*Honolulu* class), 5 DD

Issued 1700, 7 December; received 1900, 7 December
No balloons, no torpedo-defense nets deployed around battleships. No indications observed from enemy radio activity that ocean patrol flights are being made in Hawaiian area. *Lexington* left harbor yesterday (S December, local time) and recovered planes. *Enterprise* is also thought to be operating at sea with her planes on board.

Issued 1800, 7 December; received 2050, 7 December
Utah and a seaplane tender entered harbor in the evening of S December. [They had left harbor on 4 December.]
Ships in harbor as of 6 December:
9 BB, 3 CL, 3 seaplane tenders, 17 DD
In docks: 4 CL, 3 DD
All carriers and heavy cruisers are at sea. No special reports on the fleet. Oahu is quiet and Imperial General Staff is fully convinced of success.

These reports presumably had been sent from Honolulu, but I do not know the details.

On 6 December after fueling Cardin 2 and the Screening Force, the 2nd Tanker Train broke off from the task force. On the next day the 1st Tanker Train fueled the Screen again and departed. Our force then increased speed to 24 knots and raced toward Pearl Harbor. On the carrier decks planes were lined up wing to wing for their final check. Maintenance crews and flying crews worked assiduously to complete final preparation of their planes.

About this time we received Admiral Yamamoto's message for going to war: 'The rise or fall of the Empire depends upon this battle; everyone will do his duty with utmost efforts.' The message was immediately relayed to all hands, and the 'z' flag was hoisted on *Akagi*'s mast. This was the same signal flag that was run up in *Mikasa* almost thirty years before in the Straits of Tsushima.

At 1225 on the 7th (1725, 6 December in Honolulu) a message came in from submarine I-72: 'American Fleet is not in Lahaina Anchorage.'

This anchorage was used for training because it was open and deep. If the Pacific Fleet was there, it would have offered our best chance for success, and we had hoped accordingly. Receipt of the negative information, however, blasted our hopes for such an opportunity.

It was now obvious that the warships were either in Pearl Harbor or at sea. Admiral Nagumo was thumbing through the message log to check on battleships reported to be in Pearl Harbor. Completing the count, he looked up and said to the staff members, 'All of their battleships are now in. Will any of them leave today?'

The Intelligence Officer, Lieutenant Commander Ono, was first to reply: 'Since five of their eight battleships reached port on the 29th, and two others left that day returning on the 6th, there is one more which has remained in harbor all this time, supposedly under repair, or perhaps in dry dock. The five ships which arrived on the 29th have been there eight days, and it is time for them to leave. I suspect they may go out today.'

'Today is Saturday, 6 December,' said Chief of Staff Kusaka. 'Their general practice is to leave on Tuesday, which would be the 9th.'

'It is most regrettable,' said Genda, the Operations Officer, 'that no carriers are in.'

'On 29 November,' Ono explained, '*Enterprise* left harbor accompanied by two battleships, two heavy cruisers and twelve destroyers. The two battleships returned on the 6th, but the rest have not yet come back. *Lexington* came in on the 29th and left with five heavy cruisers on the 6th. Thus, *Enterprise* ought to return today. *Saratoga* is under repair at San Diego, and *Wasp* is in the Atlantic. But *Yorktown* and *Hornet* belonging to the Pacific Fleet must be out here. They may have arrived with *Enterprise* today.'

'If that happens,' said Genda, 'I don't care if all eight of the battleships are away.'

'As an air man,' remarked Oishi, 'you naturally place much importance on carriers. Of course it would be good if we could get three of them, but I think it would be better if we get all eight of the battleships.'

Chief of Staff Kusaka, who had always been strong for statistical studies of the U. S. Pacific Fleet, now spoke, 'There is only a slight chance that carriers may enter the harbor on Saturday, and it seems unlikely that the battleships would leave on Saturday or Sunday. We may take it for granted that all eight battleships will be in the harbor tomorrow. We can't do anything about carriers that are not there. I think we should attack Pearl Harbor tomorrow.'

Thus he set the stage for the decision of the task force commander, which was made known in the evening of the

7th when Admiral Nagumo gave his appraisal of the enemy situation:

1. Enemy strength in the Hawaiian area consists of eight battleships, two carriers, about ten heavy and six light cruisers. The carriers and heavy cruisers seem to be at sea, but the others are in the harbor. Those operating at sea are most likely in the training area south of Maui; they are not in Lahaina.
2. Unless an unforeseen situation develops tonight, our attack will be launched upon Pearl Harbor.
3. So far there is no indication that the enemy has been alerted, but that is no reason to relax our security.

[Number 3 says it quite clearly, Pearl Harbor was not alerted.]

At 0530, 7 December, *Chikuma* and *Tone* each catapulted a 'Zero' float plane for a pre-attack reconnaissance of Pearl Harbor. On carrier flight decks readied fighter and attack planes were lined up. The flying crews, also primed for the operation, were gathered in the briefing room. The ships pitched and rolled in the rough sea, kicking up white surf from the pre-dawn blackness of the water. At times wave spray came over the flight deck, and crews clung desperately to their planes to keep them from going into the sea.

In my flying togs I entered the operation room and reported to the Commander in Chief, 'I am ready for the mission.' Nagumo stood up, grasped my hand firmly and said, 'I have confidence in you.' He followed me to the dimly lit briefing room where *Akagi*'s Captain was waiting with the pilots. The room was not large enough for all of the men, some of whom had to stand out in the passageway. On a blackboard were written the positions of ships in Pearl Harbor as of 0600, 7 December. We were 230 miles due north of Oahu.

Calling the men to attention, I saluted Captain Hasegawa, who spoke a brief final order, 'Take off according to plan.'

The crews went out hurriedly to their waiting planes. Last to leave, I climbed to the flight deck command post where Genda put his hand on my shoulder. We smiled without speaking, knowing well each other's thoughts.

Turning to me, Air Officer Masuda said, 'There is a heavy pitch and roll. What do you think about taking off in the dark?' The sea was rough, and there was a strong wind blowing. The sky was completely dark, and as yet the horizon was not visible.

'The pitch is greater than the roll,' I replied. 'Were this a training flight, the take-off would be delayed until dawn. But if we coordinate the take-offs with the pitching we can launch successfully.' I saluted the officers and went to my plane, the tail of which was striped with red and yellow to distinguish it as the commander's.

The senior petty officer of the maintenance gang handed me a white *hachimaki* (cloth headband) saying, 'This is a present from the maintenance crews. May I ask that you take it along to Pearl Harbor?' I nodded and fastened the gift to my flying cap.

The carrier turned to port and headed into the northerly wind. The battle flag was now added to the 'z' flag flying at the masthead. Lighted flying lamps shivered with the vibration of engines as planes completed their warm-up. [At this point there was no turning back for Japan.]

On the flight deck a green lamp was waved in a circle to signal 'Take off!' The engine of the foremost fighter plane began to roar. With the ship still pitching and rolling, the plane started its run, slowly at first but with steadily increasing speed. Men lining the flight deck held their breath as the first plane took off successfully just before the ship took a downward pitch. The next plane was already moving forward. There were loud cheers as each plane rose into the air.

Thus did the first wave of 183 fighters, bombers, and torpedo planes take off from the six carriers. Within fifteen minutes they had all been launched and were forming up in the still-dark sky, guided only by signal lights of the lead planes. After one great circling over the fleet formation, the planes set course due south for Oahu Island and Pearl Harbor. It was 0615.

[This had all been set in motion with the Tanaka Memorial in 1927.]

Under my direct command were 49 level bombers. About 500 meters to my right and slightly below me were 40 torpedo planes. The same distance to my left, but about 200 meters above me, were 51 dive bombers, and flying cover for the formation there were 43 fighters. These other three groups were led by Lieutenant Commanders Murata, Takahashi, and Itaya, respectively.

We flew through and over the thick clouds which were at 2,000 meters, up to where day was ready to dawn. And the clouds began gradually to brighten below us after the brilliant sun burst into the eastern sky. I opened the cockpit canopy and looked back at the large formation of planes. The wings glittered in the bright morning sunlight.

The speedometer indicated 125 knots and we were favored by a tail wind. At 0700 I figured that we should reach Oahu in less than an hour. But flying over the clouds we could not see the surface of the water, and, consequently, had no check on our drift. I switched on the radio-direction finder to tune in the Honolulu radio station and soon picked up some light music. By turning the antenna I found the exact direction from which the broadcast was coming and corrected our course, which had been five degrees off.

Continuing to listen to the program, I was wondering how to get below the clouds after reaching Oahu. If the island was covered by thick clouds like those below us, the level bombing would be difficult; and we had not yet had reports from the reconnaissance planes.

In tuning the radio a little finer I heard, along with the music, what seemed to be a weather report. Holding my breath, I adjusted the dial and listened intently. Then I heard it come through a second time, slowly and distinctly: 'Averaging partly cloudy, with clouds mostly over the mountains. Cloud base at 3500 feet. Visibility good. Wind north, 10 knots.'

What a windfall for us! No matter how careful the planning, a more favorable situation could not have been imagined. Weather conditions over Pearl Harbor had been worrying me greatly, but now with this information I could turn my attention to other problems. Since Honolulu was only partly cloudy, there must be breaks in the clouds over the island. But since the clouds over the mountains were at 1,000 meters altitude, it would not be wise to attack from the northeast, flying over the eastern mountains, as previously planned. The wind was north and visibility good. It would be better to pass to the west of the island and make our approach from the south.

At 1030 we had been in the air for about an hour and a half. It was time that we were seeing land, but there was only a solid layer of clouds below. All of a sudden the clouds broke, and a long white line of coast appeared. We were over Kahuku Point, the northern tip of the island, and now it was time for our deployment.

There were alternate plans for the attack: If we had surprise, the torpedo planes were to strike first, followed by the level bombers and then the dive bombers, which were to attack the air bases including Hickam and Ford Island near the anchorage. If these bases were first hit by the dive bombers, it was feared that the resultant smoke might hinder torpedo and level-bombing attacks on the ships.

On the other hand, if enemy resistance was expected, the dive bombers would attack first to cause confusion and attract enemy fire. Level bombers, coming next, were to bomb and destroy enemy anti-aircraft guns, followed by the torpedo planes which would attack the ships. [Any high school student could see at this point that Pearl Harbor was wide open for attack.]

The selection of attack method was for my decision, to be indicated by signal pistol: one 'black dragon' for a surprise attack, two 'black dragons' if it appeared that surprise was lost. Upon either order the fighters were immediately to dash in as cover.

There was still no news from the reconnaissance planes, but I had made up my mind that we could make a surprise attack, and thereupon ordered the deployment by raising my signal pistol outside the canopy and firing one 'black dragon.' The time was 0740.

With this order dive bombers rose to 4,000 meters, torpedo bombers went down almost to sea level, and level bombers came down just under the clouds. The only group that failed to deploy was the fighters. Flying above the rest of the formation, they seemed to have missed the signal because of the clouds. Realizing this I fired another shot toward the fighter group. This time they noticed the signal immediately and sped toward Oahu.

This second shot, however, was taken by the commander of the dive bomber group as the second of two 'black dragons,' signifying a non-surprise attack which would mean that his group should attack first, and this error served to confuse some of the pilots who had understood the original signal.

Meanwhile, a reconnaissance report came in from *Chikuma*'s plane giving the locations of ten battleships, one heavy cruiser, and ten light cruisers in the harbor. It also reported a 14-meter wind from bearing 080, and clouds over the U. S. Fleet at 1,700 meters with a scale 7 density. The *Tone* plane also reported that 'the enemy fleet is not in Lahaina Anchorage.' Now I knew for sure that there were no carriers in the harbor. The sky cleared as we moved in on the target and Pearl Harbor was plainly visible from the northwest valley of the island. I studied our objective through binoculars. They were there all right, all eight of them. 'Notify all planes to launch attacks,' I ordered my radio man who immediately began tapping the key. The order went in plain code; '*Tora, Tora, Tora, …*' The time was 0749.

[This recon report also provided information that Pearl Harbor was ripe for an attack.]

When Lieutenant Commander Takahashi and his dive-bombing group mistook my signal, and thought we were making a non-surprise attack, his 53 planes lost no time in dashing forward. His command was divided into two groups: one led by himself which headed for Ford Island and Hickam Field, the other, led by Lieutenant Sakamoto, headed for Wheeler Field.

The dive bombers over Hickam Field saw heavy bombers lined up on the apron. Takahashi rolled his plane sharply and went into a dive, followed immediately by the rest of his planes, and the first bombs fell at Hickam. The next places hit were Ford Island and Wheeler Field. In a very short time huge billows of black smoke were rising from these bases. The lead torpedo planes were to have started their run to the Navy Yard from over Hickam, coming from south of the bay entrance. But the sudden burst of bombs at Hickam surprised Lieutenant Commander Murata who had understood that his torpedo planes were to have attacked first. Hence he took a short cut lest the smoke from those bases cover up his targets. Thus the first torpedo was actually launched some five minutes ahead of the scheduled 0800. The time of each attack was as follows:

0755 Dive bombers at Hickam and Wheeler
0757 Torpedo planes at battleships
0800 Fighters strafing air bases
0805 Level bombers at battleships

[Amazing that this is exactly what General Mitchell had predicted would happen in 1925.]

After issuance of the attack order, my level bomber group kept east of Oahu going past the southern tip of the island. On our left was the Barber's Point airfield, but, as we had been informed, there were no planes. Our information indicated that a powerful anti-aircraft battery was stationed there, but we saw no evidence of it.

I continued to watch the sky over the harbor and activities on the ground. None but Japanese planes were in the air, and there were no indications of air combat. Ships in the harbor still appeared to be asleep, and the Honolulu radio broadcast continued normally. I felt that surprise was now assured, and that my men would succeed in their missions.

Knowing that Admirals Nagumo, Yamamoto, and the General Staff were anxious about the attack, I decided that they should be informed. I ordered the following message sent to the fleet: 'We have succeeded in making a surprise attack. Request you relay this report to Tokyo.' The radio man reported shortly that the message had been received by *Akagi*.

The code for a successful surprise attack was *'Tora, Tora, Tora ...'* Before *Akagi*'s relay of this message reached Japan, it was received by *Nagata* in Hiroshima Bay and the General Staff in Tokyo, directly from my plane! This was surely a long-distance record for such a low-powered transmission from an airplane, and might be attributed to the use of the word '*Tora*' as our code. There is a Japanese saying, 'A tiger (*tora*) goes out *1,000 ri* (2,000 miles) and returns without fail.'

I saw clouds of black smoke rising from Hickam and soon thereafter from Ford Island. This bothered me and I wondered what had happened. It was not long before I saw waterspouts rising alongside the battleships, followed by more and more waterspouts. It was time to launch our level bombing attacks so

I ordered my pilot to bank sharply, which was the attack signal for the planes following us. All ten of my squadrons then formed into a single column with intervals of 200 meters. It was indeed a gorgeous formation.

The lead plane in each squadron was manned by a specially trained pilot and bombardier. The pilot and bombardier of my squadron had won numerous fleet contests and were considered the best in the Japanese Navy. I approved when Lieutenant Matsuzaki asked if the lead plane should trade positions with us, and he lifted our plane a little as a signal. The new leader came forward quickly, and I could see the smiling round face of the bombardier when he saluted. In returning the salute I entrusted the command to them for the bombing mission.

As my group made its bomb run, enemy anti-aircraft suddenly came to life. Dark gray bursts blossomed here and there until the sky was clouded with shattering near misses which made our plane tremble. Shipboard guns seemed to open fire before the shore batteries. I was startled by the rapidity of the counterattack which came less than five minutes after the first bomb had fallen. Were it the Japanese Fleet, the reaction would not have been so quick, because although the Japanese character is suitable for offensives, it does not readily adjust to the defensive.

Suddenly the plane bounced as if struck by a huge club. 'The fuselage is holed to port,' reported the radio man behind me, 'and a steering-control wire is damaged.' I asked hurriedly if the plane was under control, and the pilot assured me that it was.

No sooner were we feeling relieved than another burst shook the plane. My squadron was headed for *Nevada*'s mooring at the northern end of battleship row on the east side of Ford Island. We were just passing over the bay entrance and it was almost time to release our bombs. It was not easy to pass through the concentrated anti-aircraft fire. Flying at only 3,000 meters, it seemed that this might well be a date with eternity.

I further saw that it was not wise to have deployed in this long single-column formation. The whole level bomber group could be destroyed like ducks in a shooting gallery. It would also have been better if we had approached the targets from the direction of Diamond Head. But here we were at our targets and there was a job to be done.

It was now a matter of utmost importance to stay on course, and the lead plane kept to its line of flight like a homing pigeon. Ignoring the barrage of shells bursting around us, I concentrated on the bomb loaded under the lead plane, pulled the safety bolt from the bomb release lever and grasped the handle. It seemed as if time was standing still.

Again we were shaken terrifically and our planes were buffeted about. When I looked out the third plane of my group was abeam of us and I saw its bomb fall! That pilot had a reputation for being careless. In training his bomb releases were poorly timed, and he had often been cautioned.

I thought, 'That damn fellow has done it again!' and shook my fist in his direction. But I soon realized that there was something wrong with his plane and he was losing gasoline. I wrote on a small blackboard, 'What happened?' and held it toward his plane. He explained, 'Underside of fuselage hit.'

Now I saw his bomb cinch lines fluttering wildly, and sorry for having scolded him, I ordered that he return to the carrier. He answered, 'Fuel tank destroyed, will follow you,' asking permission to stay with the group. Knowing the feelings of the pilot and crew, I gave permission, although I knew it was useless to try taking that crippled and bombless plane through the enemy fire. It was nearly time for bomb release when we ran into clouds which obscured the target, and I made out the round face of the lead bombardier who was waving his hands back and forth to indicate that we had passed the release point. Banking slightly we turned right toward Honolulu, and I studied the anti-aircraft fire, knowing that we would have to run through it again. It was now concentrated on the second squadron.

While circling for another try, I looked toward the area in which the bomb from the third plane had fallen. Just outside the bay entrance I saw a large water ring close by what looked like a destroyer. The ship seemed to be standing in a floating dock, attached to both sides of the entrance like a gate boat. I was suddenly reminded of the midget submarines which were to have entered the bay for a special attack.

At the time of our sortie I was aware of these midget submarines, but knew nothing of their characteristics, operational objectives, force organization, or the reason for their participation in the attack. In *Akagi*, Commander Shibuya, a staff officer in charge of submarine operations, had explained that they were to penetrate the harbor the night before our attack; but, no matter how good an opportunity might arise, they were not to strike until after the planes had done so.

Even now the submarines were probably concealed in the bay, awaiting the air attack. Had the entrance been left open, there would have been some opportunity for them to get out of the harbor. But in light of what I had just seen there seemed little chance of that, and, feeling now the bitterness of war, I vowed to do my best in the assigned mission.

While my group was circling over Honolulu for another bombing attempt, other groups made their runs, some making three tries before succeeding. Suddenly a colossal explosion occurred in battleship row. A huge column of dark red smoke rose to 1,000 feet and a stiff shock wave reached our plane. I called the pilot's attention to the spectacle, and he observed, 'Yes, Commander, the powder magazine must have exploded. Terrible indeed!' The attack was in full swing, and smoke from fires and explosions filled most of the sky over Pearl Harbor.

My group now entered on a bombing course again. Studying battleship row through binoculars, I saw that the big explosion had been on *Arizona*. She was still flaming fiercely and her smoke was covering *Nevada*, the target of my group. Since the heavy smoke would hinder our bomber accuracy, I looked for some other ship to attack. *Tennessee,* third in the left row, was already on fire; but next in row was *Maryland*, which had not yet been attacked. I gave an order changing our target to this ship, and once again we headed into the anti-aircraft fire. Then came the 'ready' signal and I took a firm grip on the bomb release handle, holding my breath and staring at the bomb of the lead plane.

Pilots, observers, and radio men all shouted, 'Release!' on seeing the bomb drop from the lead plane, and all the others let go their bombs. I immediately lay flat on the floor to watch the fall of bombs through a peephole. Four bombs in perfect pattern plummeted like devils of doom. The target was so far away that I wondered for a moment if they would reach it. The bombs grew smaller and smaller until I was holding my breath for fear of losing them. I forgot everything in the thrill of watching the fall toward the target. They became small as poppy seeds and finally disappeared just as tiny white flashes of smoke appeared on and near the ship.

From a great altitude near misses are much more obvious than direct hits because they create wave rings in the water which are plain to see. Observing only two such rings plus two tiny flashes I shouted, 'Two hits!' and rose from the floor of the plane. These minute flashes were the only evidence we had of hits at that time, but I felt sure that they had done considerable damage. I ordered the bombers which had completed their runs to return to the carriers, but my own plane remained over Pearl Harbor to observe our successes and conduct operations still in progress.

[The fact that Fushida stayed to observe shows that there were no defensive measures in place.]

After our bomb run I ordered my pilot to fly over each of the air bases, where our fighters were strafing, before returning over Pearl Harbor to observe the result of our attacks on the warships. Pearl Harbor and vicinity had been turned into complete chaos in a very short time.

Target ship *Utah*, on the western side of Ford Island, had already capsized. On the other side of the island *West Virginia* and *Oklahoma* had received concentrated torpedo attacks as a result of their exposed positions in the outer row. Their sides were almost blasted off and they listed steeply in a flood of heavy oil. *Arizona* was in miserable shape, her magazine apparently having blown up, she was listing badly and burning furiously.

Two other battleships, *Maryland* and *Tennessee*, were on fire; especially the latter whose smoke emerged in a heavy black column which towered into the sky. *Pennsylvania*, unscathed in the dry-dock, seemed to be the only battleship that had not been attacked.

Most of our torpedo planes, under Lieutenant Commander Murata, flew around the Navy Yard area and concentrated their attacks on the ships moored east of Ford Island. A summary of their reports, made upon return to our carriers, indicated the following hits: one on *Nevada*, nine on *West Virginia*, twelve on *Oklahoma*, and three on *California*.

Elements of the torpedo bombers attacked ships west of the island, but they found only *Utah* and attacked her, claiming six hits. Other torpedo planes headed for *Pennsylvania*, but seeing that she was in dry-dock they shifted their attack to a cruiser and destroyer tied up at Pier 1010. Five torpedo hits were claimed on these targets, which were *Helena* and *Oglala*.

As I observed the damage done by the first attack wave, the effectiveness of the torpedoes seemed remarkable, and I was struck with the short-sightedness of the United States in being so generally unprepared and in not using torpedo nets. I also thought of our long hard training in Kagoshima Bay and the efforts of those who had labored to accomplish a seemingly impossible task. A warm feeling came with the realization that the reward of those efforts was unfolded here before my eyes.

During the attack many of our pilots noted the brave efforts of the American flyers able to take off who, though greatly outnumbered, flew straight in to engage our planes. Their effect was negligible, but their courage commanded the admiration and respect of our pilots.

It took the planes of the first attack wave about one hour to complete their mission. By the time they were headed back to our carriers, having lost three fighters, one dive bomber, and five torpedo planes, the second wave of 171 planes commanded by Lieutenant Commander Shimazaki was over the target area. Arriving off Kahuku Point at 0840, the attack run was ordered 14 minutes later and they swept in, making every effort to avoid the billowing clouds of smoke as well as the now-intensified anti-aircraft fire.

In this second wave there were 36 fighters to control the air over Pearl Harbor, 54 high-level bombers led by Shimazaki to attack Hickam Field and the Naval Air Stations at Kaneohe, while 81 dive bombers led by Lieutenant Commander Egusa flew over the mountains to the east and dashed in to hit the warships.

By the time these last arrived, the sky was so covered with clouds and smoke that planes had difficulty in locating their targets. To further complicate the problems of this attack, the ship and ground anti-aircraft fire was now very heavy. But Egusa was undaunted in leading his dive bombers through the fierce barrage. The planes chose as their targets the ships which were putting up the stiffest repelling fire. This choice proved effective since these ships had suffered least from the first attack. Thus the second attack achieved a nice spread, hitting the least damaged battleships as well as previously undamaged cruisers and destroyers. This attack also lasted about one hour, but due to the increased return fire, it suffered higher casualties: six fighters and fourteen dive bombers being lost.

After the second wave was headed back to the carriers, I circled Pearl Harbor once more to observe and photograph the results. I counted four battleships definitely sunk and three severely damaged. Still another battleship appeared to be slightly damaged and extensive damage had also been inflicted upon other types of ships. The seaplane base at Ford Island was all in flames, as were the airfields, especially Wheeler Field.

A detailed survey of damage was impossible because of the dense pall of black smoke. Damage to the airfields was not determinable, but it was readily apparent that no planes on the fields were operational. In the three hours that my plane was in the area we did not encounter a single enemy plane. It seemed that at least half the island's air strength must have been destroyed. Several hangars remained untouched, however, and it was possible that some of them held planes which were still operational.

Such were my conclusions as I prepared to return to our carrier. I was startled from these thoughts by the sudden approach of a fighter plane banking from side to side. We were greatly relieved to see the Rising Sun on its wings. As it came closer we saw that it was a *Zuikaku* fighter which must have been here since the first attack wave. I wondered if any other fighters had been left behind, and ordered my pilot to go to the rendezvous point for a final check. Sure enough, there we found a second fighter plane who also followed joyfully after us.

It was extremely difficult for fighter planes to fly long distances at sea. They were not equipped with homing devices and radar as were the larger planes. It was therefore planned to have the bombers, upon completion of their missions, rendezvous with the fighters at a designated point and lead them back to the carriers. Some of the fighters, however, such as these two, must have missed the time of rendezvous, and they were indeed fortunate to find our plane which could lead them safely back to the task force and their carriers.

[Remember that Fushida had seen that the defenses of Pearl Harbor were non-existent.]

My plane was just about the last one to get back to *Akagi*, where refueled and rearmed planes were being lined up on the busy flight deck in preparation for yet another attack. I was called to the bridge as soon as the plane stopped, and could tell on arriving there that Admiral Nagumo's staff had been engaged in heated discussions about the advisability of launching the next attack. They were waiting for my account of the battle.

'Four battleships definitely sunk,' I reported. 'One sank instantly, another capsized, the other two settled to the bottom of the bay and may have capsized.' This seemed to please Admiral Nagumo who observed, 'We may then conclude that anticipated results have been achieved.'

Discussion next centered upon the extent of damage inflicted at airfields and air bases, and I expressed my views saying, 'All things considered we have achieved a great amount of destruction, but it would be unwise to assume that we have destroyed everything. There are still many targets remaining which should be hit. Therefore I recommend that another attack be launched.'

The factors which influenced Admiral Nagumo's decision – the target of much criticism by naval experts, and an interesting subject for naval historians – have long been unknown, since the man who made it died in the summer of 1944 when United States forces invaded the Marianas. I know of only one document in which Admiral Nagumo's reasons are set forth, and there they are given as follows:

1. The first attack had inflicted all the damage we had hoped for, and another attack could not be expected to greatly increase the extent of that damage.
2. Enemy return fire had been surprisingly prompt even though we took them by surprise; another attack would meet stronger opposition and our losses would certainly be disproportionate to the additional destruction which might be inflicted.
3. Intercepted enemy messages indicated at least 50 large planes still operational; and we did not know the whereabouts of the enemy's carriers, cruisers, and submarines.
4. To remain within range of enemy land-based planes was distinctly to our disadvantage, especially since the effectiveness of our air reconnaissance was extremely limited.

I had done all I could to urge another attack, but the decision rested entirely with Admiral Nagumo, and he chose to retire without launching the next attack. Immediately flag signals were hoisted ordering the course change, and our ships headed northward at high speed.[5]

This could have been a coded message to Japanese spies living in Pearl Harbor to take cover.

Chapter XIII

FDR's Meeting with Edward Morrow and Colonel William Donovan, 1941

Of all the evidence that supports the assertion that FDR knew about the attack on Pearl Harbor, there is none more damaging than the account of the meeting he had with reporter Edward Morrow and Colonel William Donovan after the attack.

Washington
December 8, 1941
About 1:00 A.M.
During their twenty-five-minute discussion in the second-floor Oval Study, the President provided Murrow with something – we will never know exactly what – that any reporter would kill for. Long after the war ended, Murrow was asked about this meeting by author-journalist John Gunther. After a long pause, Murrow replied: 'That story would send Casey Murrow through college, and if you think I'm going to give it to you, you're out of your mind.

After he heard the first news flashes about the Pearl Harbor raid, Murrow checked with the White House to see if the supper was still on. After the Murrows were ushered into the dining room, Mrs. Roosevelt explained that the President was meeting with congressional leaders and military officers and could not join them for supper.

Throughout the evening of December 7, Roosevelt conferred with congressional and military leaders. He decided his first wartime move would come the next morning, December 8,

FDR's Meeting with Edward Morrow   189

when he would ask Congress to declare that a state of war existed between Japan and the United States. He prepared a rough draft of what later became his 'Day of Infamy' speech. Then he invited Murrow and Donovan into the study for a midnight snack of sandwiches and cold beer.

Only Donovan has hinted at what went on: the conversation was mostly about public reaction to the attack. He sensed that this was FDR's overriding concern. The President asked Murrow and Donovan whether they thought the attack was a clear case of a first Japanese move that would unite Americans behind a declaration of war against the Axis powers. Both guests thought it would indeed have that effect.

Donovan believed that Roosevelt welcomed the attack and that it was less of a surprise to him than it was to others in the White House. FDR claimed he sent an advance warning to Pearl Harbor that an attack by Japan was imminent.

Several years later Murrow made a brief, circumspect broadcast that in part addressed the question of what the President had known before the Japanese hit Pearl Harbor.[1]

The information that was exchanged in that meeting will never be known. The fact is that neither Morrow and Donovan gave a full account of what Roosevelt said about what he knew about Pearl Harbor, although he told both men exactly what he knew and what happened. There was no minutes kept in this meeting, and there should be no doubt in any historian's mind that FDR swore these two men to keep the secrets of what was said in this meeting. These are the facts of this meeting, it is up to the historian to try and clarify what took place.

Though some authors (not true historians or scholars) try to cover up the true historical importance of this meeting, they cannot.

CBS correspondent Edward R. Murrow had a dinner appointment at the White House on 7 December. Because of the attack he and his wife only ate with Mrs. Roosevelt, but the president asked Murrow to stay afterwards. As he waited outside the Oval Office, Murrow observed government and military officials entering and leaving. He wrote after the war:

There was ample opportunity to observe at close range the bearing and expression of Mr. Stimson, Colonel Knox, and Secretary Hull. If they were *not* surprised by the news from Pearl Harbor, then that group of elderly men were putting on a performance which would have excited the admiration of any experienced actor ... It may be that the degree of the disaster had appalled them and that they had known for some time ... But I could not believe it then and I cannot do so now. There was amazement and anger written large on most of the faces.

[This is used by journalists and historians and scholars to try and say they did not know, but this is completely wrong. They were not angry because of the attack, they were angry that the attack by the Imperial Japanese Navy had been so effective. They knew the attack was coming, this is what they were so angry about not the attack itself. But these FDR lovers do everything they can to keep covering up for the President.]

One historian has written, however, that when Murrow met Roosevelt with William J. Donovan of the OSS that night, while the magnitude of the destruction at Pearl Harbor horrified the president, Roosevelt seemed slightly less surprised by the attack than the other men. According to Murrow, the president told him, 'Maybe you think [the attack] didn't surprise us!' He said later, 'I believed him', and thought that he might have been asked to stay as a witness. When allegations of Roosevelt's foreknowledge appeared after the war, John Gunther asked Murrow about the meeting. Murrow reportedly responded the full story would pay for his son's college education and 'if you think I'm going to give it to you, you're out of your mind'. Murrow did not write the story, however, before his death.[2]

That last statement by Edward Murrow is what is so powerful about that meeting. Again this point's to the fact that FDR knew the attack was coming and when it was to take place. The information that has been amassed from 1925 to 7 December 1941 proves beyond a

FDR's Meeting with Edward Morrow 191

shadow of doubt that FDR and his staff along with the Washington D.C. military intelligence staff knew the date the attack was coming. The other amazing thing to consider is why were Kimmel and Short, the commanders at Pearl Harbor, not court-martialled for dereliction of duty, even though all eyes were on them during this time. The questions should be asked, 'Was this a way to deflect from the fact that FDR, Marshall and Stark knew the attack was coming?' and 'Were Admiral Kimmel and General Short involved with FDR in knowing of the attack?' This would definitely seem like a possibility since it was Kimmel who gave the order to the carrier fleet on Friday, 5 December to stay out to sea and not return until Monday, 8 December. Every historian knows that carriers were what Admiral Yamamoto wanted destroyed in his attack.

The question must also be asked: 'Why did Admiral Kimmel not deploy the torpedo nets in the harbor?' This would have surely have helped to defend he many ships against the torpedoes being dropped from the Japanese planes. Then, of course, the next question that must be asked is, 'Why after the American destroyer attacked and sunk the Japanese mini submarine (at 3:42 am a Japanese mini sub was spotted by the mine sweeper USS *Condor* and reported to HQ at Pearl Harbor), which was over three and a half hours before the attack, why was the naval base not immediately put on full alert?' These questions are still unanswered today. To any of the relatives who had soldiers, sailors or marines die at Pearl Harbor (and the Philippines, for this attack was followed by one there) let me say that the American government owes you a huge apology for allowing this atrocity to happen when it could have well been prevented. The one person who bears the most blame for allowing this to happen is FDR.

The simple fact is that after the sinking of the USS *Panay* on the Yangtze, along with the Nanking Massacre, an atrocity as horrific as those seen in Nazi Germany (and in the Pacific the USA was not practising isolationism), FDR should have declared war on the Imperial Japanese Government for these acts of war. That he did not is a crime in itself.

Chapter XIV

1941 to Present: The United States Cover-up

The amazing thing about the attack on Pearl Harbor is that more than eighty years after the attack, the United States still has thousands upon thousands of documents classified as 'Top Secret' and it does not look like they will get released anytime soon. Most of the documents that have been released thanks to the Freedom of Information Act (FOIA) have been redacted to the point that an individual cannot read them anyway. Both the Democratic and Republican parties are to blame.

During the late 1970s President Jimmy Carter released very little information on Pearl Harbor, and most of the documents he did release were redacted. One radio message, issued by Admiral Yamamoto and Emperor Hirohito, announced the intentions of the Imperial Japanese government for war on 6 December 1941. This was in the early part of the morning on Saturday Hawaiian time. This message was intercepted in Hawaii but it was never delivered to Kimmel or Short over the next twenty-six hours. An English version of this message was released by President Carter. However, the original two-part message that is in the Japanese language and the codes that were used to decode it are listed as 'Top Secret' and contained under the ruse of national security. The question that must be asked after eighty years, is why?

However, the true intercept details of the Hirohito-Yamamoto dispatch can today be found in the Station H Logs that our government forgot to classify as 'Top Secret'. The message is so powerful that if it had been heard at the Tokyo War Crimes Tribunal it would have been enough to bring Emperor Hirohito to justice for the war crimes he committed. The dispatch was was sent to the Combined Fleet and urged the officers and men to completely annihilate the enemy. This message was presented to the commanders of the combined fleet and Yamamoto told his commanders he had received it on 2 December 1941. This message was sent to all commanders at 4.30 a.m. on 6 December Hawaiian time. This message was transmitted through the Pacific to all Japanese units. The radio operators intercepted these messages and decoded them directly off the naval airwaves.

'There is an enormous amount of intercepts and documents still sequestered by the Defense Department as Top Secret classification, and the Hirohito-Yamamoto is only one of them. Only the English version has been released with its misleading information that conforms to the cover-up. None of the 7 messages that were prepared by the radio operators and decoders of these messages has ever been declassified.'[1] The fact that none of these messages will probably ever be released for the American public to read shows how corrupt our own government is today and has been since 1941.

The best way to understand this is to realise that President Carter only released the American version of the 'Climb Mount Niitaka' message. 'The original Japanese intercept, obtained by Joseph Christie Howard, produced at least two official Navy documents on 8½ x 11 paper. The Navy has censored Howard and his original records. Though he was America's expert witness to the 'Climb Niitaka' message, he never testified before any Pearl Harbor investigation.'[2] The apparent conclusion should be that the President does not have the authority or the power to declassify documents from eighty years ago on Pearl Harbor. President Trump could not do it and President Biden cannot do it. FDR made sure that these documents would never be seen by the American public to show his treason in sacrificing young men at Pearl Harbor and the Philippines to keep his image intact as a great president. This fallacy needs to come to an end. President Truman's resolution to keep documents pertaining to Pearl Harbor Top Secret needs to be rescinded and these documents released to the American public. With the National Security Act of 1947 the United States government decides what we get to know.

A Gallup poll in 1991 revealed that one in three Americans believed that President Franklin Roosevelt knew about the eventual attack on Pearl Harbor beforehand. Today almost 85 per cent believe that FDR knew when and where the attack was going to take place.

As further evidence there is a series of deciphered messages back and forth from Japanese and American parties in the months leading up to the attack. Most of these messages are from the Japanese to their fleets and back. I found them housed at the Fordham University website, but they can be found in many places on the web. These messages largely consist of Japanese scouting or recon:

> From: Tokyo To: Pearl Harbor Attack Force Date: 2 DEC 1941
> 'Climb Mount Niitaka.'

This was the message that would tell the fleet commander to open sealed documents that would give him his orders.

> From: Adm. Nagumo To: Pearl Harbor Attack Force Date: 3 Dec. 1941
> 1. 'It has already been ordered to go to war on 8 December, but so critical has become the situation in the Far East that one can hardly predict war would not explode by that time. So far no new information on Hawaii area received and also no indications of our Task Force being detected. But since the enemy intention is naturally far beyond prediction, strict attention will be directed to meet any unexpected encounter with an enemy.'
> 2. 'It is intended that this force will operate as scheduled even if war breaks out before 8 December.'

Admiral Nagumo was the Japanese Navy's carrier strike force commander, and the Pearl Harbor Attack Force was the fleet en route to attack on 8 December in Japan (7 December in the U.S.).

1941 to Present: The United States Cover-up 195

A letter from Lt John Leitweiler, Commander of Station CAST, Corregidor in Manila, to Lt Lee W. Parke, Chief, Japanese Cryptography Section, U.S. Navy, on 16 November 1941 states that his team is current and complete in deciphering all current interceptions from the Japanese. His team was kept steadily busy, but they were able to keep up. It is this letter that allows us to be confident that the code breaking was moving efficiently. Even more important, however, is the fact that the letter very clearly indicates that Parke was vehemently and frequently trying to force poor methods upon his teams, seemingly in an effort to disrupt the efficient operations. Leitweiler goes on to admonish his superior for trying to force these much slower techniques upon him.

The Hawaiian office of the American Red Cross received enormous amounts of supplies just days before the attack on Pearl Harbor despite public conversations about peace and isolationism by Congress and the American people, as found in the Hawaii War Records department. Why were these supplies sent to Pearl Harbor if the base was considered the most unlikely of attack points? Because, as noted above on 3 December, the U.S. already knew the attack was going to happen.

As late as 1995 more information about what FDR knew and secret documents were being released through the FOIA. Further, a letter from Helen Hamman, daughter of Don C. Smith, to President Clinton in 1995 sought to clear up a fight to posthumously change the ranks of the Pearl Harbor commanders. Smith served as Director of the War Service for the Red Cross. His daughter related:

> Shortly before the attack in 1941 President Roosevelt called [Smith] to the White House for a meeting concerning a Top Secret matter. At this meeting the President advised my father that his intelligence staff had informed him of a pending attack on Pearl Harbor, by the Japanese. He anticipated many casualties and much loss. He instructed my father to send workers and supplies to a holding area at a [port of entry] on

the West Coast where they would await further orders to ship out, no destination was to be revealed. He left no doubt in my father's mind that none of the Naval and Military officials in Hawaii were to be informed and he was not to advise the Red Cross officers who were already stationed in the area. When he protested to the President, President Roosevelt told him that the American people would never agree to enter the war in Europe unless they were attack [sic] within their own borders.[3]

All this information was declassified after the Gallup poll that showed 85 per cent of Americans believed that Pearl Harbor was not a surprise attack, and we should expect that the number today would be higher. Even so, many journalists will argue loudly that it is a theory and that there is no evidence to support the proposal that FDR would use the attack on Pearl Harbor as a way of getting the U.S. into a war that he repeatedly argued in Washington that the U.S. needed to be in. It is extremely difficult to believe that anyone can view these presented facts and argue anything other than an invitation to war was presented by FDR to Hideki Tojo.

The mere fact that Japan already had spies in the United States as early as the 1920s gives even more credence to the 'the Tanaka Memorial', since according to this document it was in Japan's future to eventually conquer the United States and it was presented to the Emperor in 1927. The information in the above article was not discovered until 2018 buried in the Library of Congress and the FBI files. It almost sounds redundant, but as they used to say on *The X-Files*, the truth is out there. The historian needs only to be thorough in the way he does his research to come up with the truth. The information shows that FDR had to know of the attack, so yes he is guilty of treason and even though he has been dead for over seventy years he should be tried in a Military Court of Law since he was the Commander in Chief of the United States at the time of Pearl Harbor.

The documents that have been presented stated that war between the U.S and Japan was inevitable and nothing was going to stop it.

The fact is that all of these newly released documents from 1985 to the present have stood the test of time. Even with the ranting and raving of FDR journalists and scholars who try to cover up the truth, they no longer can. As each day goes by and more and more evidence is mounted against FDR and his commanders, it will eventually be proven beyond a doubt that FDR was guilty of treason. The American people want the truth about this event, and they deserve the truth of the complicity of FDR in the war with Japan. For all those heroes who died at Pearl Harbor, the citizens of the USA salute you.

Chapter XV

Conclusion

To begin with, this is a book of facts. The events detailed within it in all took place. There is no doubt that Japan wanted to go to war with the United States. This fact can be seen by the spies they had working in the United States as early as the 1920s through to the recently uncovered files of the Federal Bureau of Investigation (FBI) along with the Tanaka Memorial, which more and more historians and scholars are now viewing as a real document. Along with the evidence from Japan's spies in Hawaii through the 1930s, this proves the point beyond a shadow of a doubt.

Two principles of Japanese conduct contributed to the militaristic expansionist policy of Japan (from as early as 1927), hakko ichiu and kodo. The first means making the world one big family. The second means the national policy of Japan made hakko ichiu the moral goal and kodo the way to achieve it. In actuality, the militarists were following the ideas published in a book by Dr. Shumei Okawa in 1924 where Okawa argued that 'since Japan had been the first state in existence, it was Japan's divine mission to rule the world.' [The Tanaka Memorial plan for world conquest, again amazing that scholars and journalist do not see this connection.] Japanese civilians were repeatedly told that the Japanese were the master race and their mission was to 'end the tyrannical rule and oppression of the westerners.' The next step in the expansionist policy was the suppression of freedom of speech and censorship of all written material. As Japan's conquest of Asian colonies began, it was clear from the start this would not be one big happy family. In each of the places captured by the Japanese, civilians and prisoners were murdered, tortured, bayoneted, beaten, and raped. Then in 1928 [One year after the Tanaka Memorial was presented to the Emperor], Japan's Kwantung army secretly assassinated Marshall Chang Tso-lien, the warlord of the great, mineral-rich territory of Manchuria [exactly what the Tanaka Memorial said they would do] that bordered Korea. The action was made quite easy since Japan had annexed Korea in 1910 and could move freely across the border.

The assassination was a major coup on the part of the army and Colonel Daisaku Komoto, senior staff officer, planned the explosion that killed Marshall Chang. The Emperor, to save face at the time, rebuked Minister Giichi Tanaka [a ploy], having him resign [another ploy], and appointed Osachi Hamaguchi prime minister. Then in 1930, Prime Minister Hamaguchi was assassinated. The assassin was made a hero in the Japanese press for killing an unpatriotic leader and also led to many more killings of the Hamaguchi cabinet.[1]

So as any scholar can come to realise with critical thinking that the Tanaka Memorial was a real document.

To the many scholars who try and dismiss the Tanaka Memorial because they say they cannot find any reference to it in the Japanese Archives, they seem to forget that Japan destroyed thousands of documents during the war to cover up the crimes that they committed. The best example of this is the Palawan Massacre of Allied PoWs in the Philippines, which we know happened due to the few men who survived it. However, there is not a single document of this massacre in the Japanese Archives. This is the most mundane argument that scholars from the 1980s and 1990s would use to say the Tanaka Memorial was a fake. This is ludicrous. There is more than enough evidence to prove the Memorial document is real. As with the war crimes they committed before the war had even ended, Japanese Imperial Government had already ordered the destroying of documents that could prove them guilty of these war crimes in January 1945.

Even now Japan is still trying to deny these crimes, which the world knows took place. Do not forget that they also honor their war criminals with the Yasukuni Shrine, which has the names of men who raped and murdered women and children as heroes. They also censor their history books to make sure their children do not learn of these war crimes. So they do not even teach true history. They even have lobbyists in the United States fighting to keep this information hidden. So you cannot trust the Japanese Government on this matter. So, of course, a historian will not find documents in the Japanese Archives. It is that simple.

Then there is the problem of Southeast Asia/Vietnam. Since very few wartime records have survived from Vietnam the world may never truly know how many atrocities the Imperial Japanese Army committed there. The number of killings of women and children in Vietnam could be in the millions. If the atrocities match what they did in the Philippines and China, it is not hard for the historian to consider that this could have happened. One only has to look at France, which was in Vietnam as a colony, but pulled out and refused to defend it when Japan invaded.

> Here is an entirely different kind of topic that requires scrutiny. Why was the army of Vichy France willing and able to fight everyone on the face of the earth except Germany, Japan, and Italy? In 1940, at the same time as the army at Dakar was fighting the British and the Free French, the army in northern Indo-China was not called on to defend the French Colony against Japan! In the summer of 1941 the French army in Syria fought against the British, the Australians, and the Free French; at the same time, there was no resistance to the Japanese occupation in Vietnam (the United States would send in OSS agents to train and help the Vietnamese fight the Japanese.)

In early 1942, the Vichy government urged the Germans to agree to joint efforts to try and get the Japanese to land on Madagascar. When American soldiers landed in Northwest Africa in November of 1942, hundreds of American soldiers were killed by French bullets; but not one German or Italian soldier was as much as scratched when they landed in Tunisia or occupied the unoccupied portion of France. The literature on Vichy deals with each of these incidents in isolation without ever putting them together, without considering the general pattern which is so extraordinary. The French forces in all these events were commanded by leaders who had made their way up the promotion ladder in pre-war years.[2]

All of these soldiers should have been charged with war crimes, but this was not the case, very few were. Then of course, do not forget that the American Army had OSS agents in Vietnam assisting the Vietnamese in fighting the Japanese. OSS Officer Austin Glass put it best about the French:

> I do not believe that the French have ever understood the Annamese mentality, because they have been, for the most part, too egotistical and avaricious to comprehend the aspirations of other peoples. The liberty which they claim for themselves, they deny others. They talk much of French dignity but they frequently treat the people under them with a callous disregard for human rights and dignity. The semi-slavery of the plantation coolies, the corralling of peasants for forced labor on dykes, roads, etc., or the induction into a native army for slave labor, are all cases in point. The world has recently been horrified by the French in their attempt to dominate the Syrians; but that is what they have been doing in Indo-China for nearly 100 years.[3]

So, as this OSS officer said, and this historian agrees, do not trust the French. Americans should remember that it was France that pushed for the First World War, the treaties of France and the United Kingdom at the end of that war was the direct cause of the Second World War, and at the end of the war, France – which would not even defend Vietnam – wanted it back as its colony, which is what caused the Vietnam War. Think of all the Americans who died due to France's culpability. And historians should remember this: many American soldiers died at the hands of the Vichy French in North Africa during World War II! U.S. Army Rangers fought tenaciously under the command of Lt Colonel William Darby at Arzew, Algeria, against Vichy France in late November 1942.

This could have all been stopped by FDR if he had only declared war on Japan after the sinking of the *Panay* in 1937. The historian needs to remember that FDR knew of the atrocities the Japanese were committing in the Pacific and did nothing to stop them. He also knew of the French atrocities to the Vietnam people even before Japan arrived and allowed these to happen. France should have been kicked out of Vietnam in the 1930s, which would have prevented the Vietnam War. Japan invading and committing atrocities in Vietnam, the French allowed to happen. It was America that sent in OSS agents to help Vietnam fight the Japanese. If FDR had declared war on Japan in 1937, which he had every right to do so, then the atrocities in China, Vietnam and the Philippines would never have happened. FDR and the French can share the blame for all the Japanese atrocities that took place in Vietnam. The French did not even raise one single defence in defending Vietnam, and as this book has shown, FDR did not care as his main goal was to get the United States into a war with Japan no matter what the cost in human lives and atrocities.

Even in the United States, the Japanese use their influence to hide their war crimes, as was seen in a previous chapter. They also shot down a resolution in 2006 to bring Japan to answer for its war crimes. Even Japanese Americans want answers to this. On 22 September 2006 twenty-five congressional co-sponsors of the measure, including Mike

Honda of California, the leading Japanese American in Congress, sent a letter to Hastert & Boehner asking them to bring the resolution to the floor before Congress adjourned for the November elections.'[4] Yet they would not, so the resolution was never voted on. The Japanese lobbyists had seen to that. So again, even to this date Japan hides its war crimes and honors its war criminals.

The historian needs to remember that this is the Japanese Government, not the Japanese people. Many Japanese want the truth to be told, yet their government does not allow them. The Japanese people of today are honorable people. Yet even today Japan does not teach any of the history of the atrocities that its Imperial Japanese Government of the Second World War committed to its school children, and even documents of these atrocities have disappeared from the records in the Japanese Archives.

This should make any scholar aware that the only thing in Japan's archives is what the Japanese Government wants the historian to see. Documents on Unit 731 (not in the Japanese Archives), the Tanaka Memorial (not in the Japanese Archives), the Nanking Massacre (not in the Japanese Archives), the Palawan Massacre (not in the Japanese Archives), Manila Massacre (not in the Japanese Archives), and the treatment of Allied PoWs have all disappeared or were never put in the Japanese Archives. Not one of the leaflets that President Truman dropped on the cities to be targeted with the A-bomb warning the citizens to leave can be found in the Japanese Archives.

An excellent document that did survive, although not in Japan, is one titled August 1 Kill-All Order concerning Allied PoWs, which reads:

> When the battle situation becomes urgent the POWs will be concentrated and confined in their location and kept under heavy guard until preparations for the final disposition will be made. Although the basic aim is to act under superior orders, individual disposition may be made in certain circumstances. Whether they are destroyed individually or in groups, and whether it is

accomplished by means of mass bombing, poisonous smokes, poisons, drowning, or decapitation, dispose of them as the situation dictates. It is the aim not to allow the escape of a single one, to annihilate them all, and not to leave any traces.[5]

The Japanese did this at Palawan with 150 PoWs but eleven escaped. All were wounded but they did survive; the others were burned or machine-gunned. This document was to be destroyed, but luckily a copy did survive (not in the Japanese Archives, but in the American National Archives). All the other documents have been destroyed. This makes it extremely hard to find documents that no longer exist in Japan, so the historian has to look elsewhere. This should be a warning to any historian and journalist that the Japanese Archives are flawed in dealing with its atrocities.

Even if Japan had not attacked Pearl Harbor, it would have eventually attacked the United States as the documents, in the previous chapters have proven. The point that this book has set out to prove, however, is that it was not a surprise attack by the Imperial Japanese Navy but one that was helped set in motion by FDR and his commanders. The President had been pushing Japan to attack the United States in early 1940 to get the country into the war as soon as possible. Since war had broken out in Europe in 1939 FDR – more concerned about being re-elected –would need the United States to be attacked and many die to get his country into the war, yet this should not have been the case. The *Panay* incident was more than enough reason for the United States to go to war with Japan in 1937. FDR was more concerned with his own political ambition than the American people.

The *Panay* incident was an unprovoked attack on an American gunship and convoy that killed many American sailors and civilians. Records show that the convoy had been in touch with Japanese officials while they were trying to leave on the Yangtze River, and stayed in touch until the attack. A film was made showing it was a deliberate attack. FDR put forth the idea that it was the result of reckless flying by the Japanese pilots and was an accident, which he knew was a lie at the time. Again this is a treasonous act for Americans were killed and no action was taken.

Then of course during this same time the Nanking Massacre took place. Photos were smuggled out and given to FDR and he did nothing about it. This is a huge dark historical stain on America's past. The argument that the United States was practising isolationism does not hold water in the Pacific War, for the US had Army and Navy personnel in the Philippines, Hawaii, Guam, and even until the end of 1937 gun boats on the Yangtze River in China. There was no isolation there. At this point it should have been clear to any high-ranking commander in the United States military that Japan was going to eventually declare war on the United States.

Then of course, FDR did not beef up the military in the Philippines. Instead, he kept sending military equipment to Europe, leaving America's young men to defend the Philippines with outdated war surplus. So anyone who had relatives die at Pearl Harbor or in the Philippines due to FDR's lacklustre approach to Japan at this time should look at the President as the failure he was. The fact that a historian or scholar must remember is that the *Panay* incident and the Nanking Massacre happened in 1937, which gave FDR more than ample time to beef up the United States' defences in Pearl Harbor and the Philippines, but he did not.

The other problem is that FDR became friends and allies with Joseph Stalin, a dictator who had over 20 million of his own people murdered, making him a bigger mass murderer than Hitler. Hitler knew this and that is why he had no problem deciding to invade the Soviet Union, for he knew Stalin had killed over 90 per cent of his premier officers and this left him with untrained and untested officers. FDR knew Stalin was a mass murder before Hitler. Then, of course, our government today wants to be friends with China and the Maoist regime that since 1948 has killed an estimated 50 million of its own people, making it the biggest group of murderers of all time.

Then you have the naval war games in Pearl Harbor in 1932 and 1938 that showed how defenseless the U.S. Navy and Army was, yet none of FDR's commanders paid heed to them. And of course, the final exam question, asked of Japanese naval cadets before they could graduate, starting in 1935, was: 'How would you conduct a surprise attack on Pearl Harbor?' This should have been a red flag to FDR or any of his commanders for their spies had reported this back to them. Then again, they might have chosen to ignore this historical question to allow the attack on Pearl Harbor. There is no doubt that they did.

The problem is that FDR did everything he could to get Japan to attack as soon as possible by placing restrictions on the Japanese government. The FBI knew that there were Japanese spies in America and Hawaii reporting back to Japan as early as the 1920s. The true smoking gun, however, is the Lieutenant Commander Arthur McCollum memo of October 1940 that provided FDR eight actions to conduct that would lead Japan to attack the United States in quick time. Then, of course, FDR put these actions into effect.

Then do not forget that FDR approved the 'pop up' cruises, officially known as Action D, in Japanese waters to try and entice Japan into attacking the U.S. Navy ships starting in March 1941 through to July 1941. FDR did not care if Japan sank the cruisers and destroyers with the possibility of over 3,000 men's lives lost, it would draw Japan into a war with the United States. This should wake up scholars and historians to the fact that FDR allowed the attack on Pearl Harbor to happen. It does not take rocket science to understand this.

Then there are all the documents that have been uncovered from intercepts of the Imperial Japanese Navy, along with all the top-secret messages sent by Washington D.C.'s commanders that have been found. However, remember there are thousands of other documents that are still classified as 'Top Secret' that have not been released. Even without those documents, there are more than enough documents to prove, as this book has, that FDR knew of the attack on Pearl Harbor, the date and year. The other thing that needs to be remembered by historians and scholars is that right after the attack on Pearl Harbor, FDR ordered thousands of documents destroyed, so according to his ruse, they would not fall into Japanese hands if they made it to Washington D.C.. First off, if Japan had made it into Washington D.C., it would have been over for the United States, for the war would have definitely been lost if that had happened. This lemon should have never been bought by the American public. This was FDR and his commanders in Washington D.C. covering themselves.

The other problem that is obvious here is that if Pearl Harbor was such a great blunder by Admiral Kimmel and General Short, why were they not court-martialled? In 1999 the United States Senate passed a resolution saying that Short and Kimmel performed their duties competently and professionally. Really? This is ludicrous, as the previous chapters of this book have pointed out. Then President Clinton ignored the letter sent to him by the daughter of the head of the Red Cross at the time of Pearl Harbor that proved FDR knew the attack was coming and when it was coming. A historian must remember that Japanese Admiral Yamamoto was after the U.S. carriers, and now America knows that on Friday, 5 December 1941 Kimmel sent memos to each carrier fleet to stay out of Pearl Harbor until Monday, 8 December. Anyone could tell you from this information that Kimmel and Short were part of FDR's plan to allow Japan to attack Pearl Harbor on 7 December. So historians and scholars who still support the notion that this was a sneak attack are clearly in error.

The warnings were there, they are impossible to deny, as are the documents, of which most can be found in the United States Library of Congress. The problem is that there are historians, scholars and journalists who only want to promote the original story of the attack on Pearl Harbor when if they just would carry out proper research they would come to understand just what a liar that FDR was to the American people. The NSA is part of the problem in that they keep thousands of documents as top secret and the American public never knows the truth about a historical event.

The information is there to bring Franklin D. Roosevelt and his staff up on treason charges. Unfortunately it is too late for that, for they are all dead. However, historians and scholars can now tell the truth for they can research the evidence and come to an easy conclusion as to what took place during this historical event. The main reason this needs to be done is that Americans need to know the truth. When the government lies to the American people, then they do a dishonor to the young men who gallantly fought and died to preserve our freedoms.

The relatives of these men need to know that they were not sacrificed for a good reason. As was pointed out before, America should have been at war with Japan in 1937. America should have to answer to the relatives of these young men as to why it still covers up the truth and does not release all the documents it has on Pearl Harbor. It is coming up on eighty years and there are still thousands of documents still classified on the grounds of national security. This is a travesty!

As a historian scholar, I do not believe in coincidences. The one thing that is an absolute is that they do not happen in major amounts. Any physics professor will tell you this. A mathematics professor friend of mine at a southern university did a study of what the odds of all these incidents involving Pearl Harbor from 1925 up to 7 December 1941 were of being a coincidence and he came up with what is called a 'magnitude of zero', which means the odds are so great that it was impossible for it to have taken place without FDR knowing it. However, many of our historians and scholars today still want to perpetrate the fallacy that the attack on Pearl Harbor was a sneak attack.

Since Robert Stinnett (RIP) wrote his book *Day of Deceit* in 2000 in which he proposed that FDR and his staff knew that Pearl Harbor was going to be attacked, hundreds of new documents have been found. In this book I have only included a small number of these documents that deal with Pearl Harbor and the Philippines. Included also were documents on Unit 731, to show how papers were kept secret from the American public from 1945 until the 1990s on this unit. One must remember that there are no documents on Unit 731 in the Japanese

Archives, which goes to prove that they cannot be trusted. Even back in 1943, when the only successful escape from a Japanese PoW camp was made at Davao in the Philippines by ten Americans, FDR would cover this up for as long as he could. The escapees told of the Bataan Death March, which he already knew about in 1942 from the 'Bamboo Telegraph' in the Philippines, but acted surprised when these men spoke of it. When Major William Dyess, one of the PoWs who escaped, wanted to tell his story, he was blocked from talking to the press. 'Indiana Representative Gerald Landis told Congress and the Senate in the year of 1944 President Roosevelt and Harry Hopkins (the major policy maker behind the Lend-Lease Act) are directly responsible for not getting supplies to General MacArthur in the Philippines that would have saved these men's lives in 1940 and 1941.'[6] (One of Major Dyess's fellow escapees was 1st Lt Austin Shofner, a former University of Tennessee football player who credited Tennessee football coach Brigadier General Robert Neyland and his coaching principles with his ability to survive.)

If the American and Japanese governments do not come clean about their actions in the Second World War involving all the events discussed in this book, then it is not just the American and Japanese people that will suffer but also future generations. It has been said by many a historian and scholar that 'History is a fable agreed upon!' It does not mean that the history that is taught to the student of history is true. This is a statement students of history should always remember.

In this concluding chapter the use of the atomic bombs on Hiroshima and Nagasaki and whether or not they actually saved lives – both Japanese and American – must be discussed. The answer to this question is simple: yes they did. Should they be considered as a war crime? Again the answer is simple; no they should not. The argument that Japan would have surrendered is just a fallacy. The Emperor had no intention of surrendering until after the use of the bombs. He was siding with the military commanders on this. One only has to read the book by historian George Feifer, *The Battle of Okinawa*, where in his final chapters he discusses this historical act.

Then there is the case of Imperial Japanese Naval Commander Fushida, the pilot who led the way for the attack on Pearl Harbor, who was asked in the late 1950s how he felt about America dropping the bombs. He told the reporter that he was glad America dropped the bombs because it ended the war, for the Japanese Imperialist would have kept on fighting until the whole country of Japan was annihilated. As one Japanese historian put it, without the bombs, the Japanese race might have ceased to exist.

Many historians want to argue that Japanese civilians living at the time the bombs were dropped say that this was an atrocity. They actually saw the bombs as a godsend, for it ended the war. 'That's why many Japanese civilians cheered the bomb! Not surprisingly, the Japanese kept their approval to themselves. After a half century later, few feel able to voice their belief that the terrible weapon liberated them. But to this day, non-militarists Japanese, of which there were millions, now and then do whisper a confession that they believed they were doomed before Hiroshima and Nagasaki saved them.'[7]

One only has to look at what a Nagasaki survivor said: 'A highly intelligent but otherwise fairly typical young woman living in a village very near Nagasaki never thought of surrender until then because it was unimaginable. (Failure to attend her school's special class in use of the bamboo spear would have led to court arrest.) Although deeply grateful to the bomb for 'doing the trick' of saving her, she could not express that because she lost so many friends in Nagasaki and it would have 'looked indecent.' But she had no doubt that the bomb gave her leaders a way out. Now she could hope that 'maybe there was a future of a kind instead of no future, thank god!'[8] These bombs would force the Emperor along with the politicians of the Imperial Japanese government to surrender.

If historians and scholars were to consider the question: 'Would there have been a way to avoid the use of the atomic bomb?' they should concentrate on the year 1937 and FDR. This is the year that America should have gone to war with Japan. If FDR had behaved like Hitler and, when he took office in 1933, concentrated on building American arms for the U.S. Navy and Army in the Pacific then in 1937 when

Japan attacked the *Panay*, America could have swooped in on Japan and wiped out their Navy and Army so quickly that Japan would not have been able to make war. If FDR had done this there would have been no attack on Pearl Harbor or the Philippines, and the Bataan Death March would have never taken place (these three incidents are an absolute), and no need for the use of the atomic bomb. This would have also stopped Japan becoming allied to Nazi Germany, thus also allowing America to come to a swift aid to Europe against Hitler and Nazi Germany with the possibility of ending the war in 1943 with millions of lives saved. This myth of FDR being a great President needs to end! The Japanese spies of the 1920s; General Mitchell's 1925 warning; the Tanaka Memorial 1927; the 1935 question to Japanese Naval Cadets to graduate; the Nanking Massacre of 1937–38 and finally the attack on the *Panay* in 1937 were more than ample enough reasons to go to war with Japan in 1938, no matter how you slice it! The fact that FDR sacrificed the soldiers, sailors, and marines lives at Pearl Harbor and then in the Philippines makes him guilty of treason.

The reason as a historian that I have pointed out in this final chapter all the atrocities that were committed by the Japanese: the Nanking Massacre, Unit 731, the Comfort Women, the attack on Pearl Harbor, the Bataan Death March, the Manila Massacre, the treatment of Allied PoWs, and the Palawan Massacre, along with the use of the atomic bombs, and even including the French and the Vietnam War, is the fact that none of this may have even come to pass if FDR had declared war on Japan after the sinking of the *Panay*.

This has been a book of facts. It is left up to the reader to come to their own conclusion as to how they determine these facts. One final note that must be considered: when researching the documents on FDR and Pearl Harbor, many of the documents I found in the Library of Congress and National Archives were redacted and could not be used. Their contents are still deemed to be a threat to national security but the question must be asked is why after nearly eighty years do they need to be considered in this way? The American public needs to finally know the truth. In a previous chapter it was reported that Japan hides the truth about its war atrocities from its students and even has a shrine that honors the war criminals who committed the atrocities outlined in this book. However, the United States should consider whether it is doing the same thing by hiding the truth about FDR and the attack on Pearl Harbor. This is something that needs to be rectified.

The students of history need to study the real truth about history instead of history that is written by politicians and the media. Military philosopher Carl von Clausewitz wrote:

> Of course, we must not be satisfied with history's main conclusions, and still less with the reason of historians, but we must penetrate as deeply as possible into the details. For the aim of historians rarely is to present the absolute truth. Usually they wish to embellish the deeds of their army or to demonstrate the concordance of events with imaginary rules. They invent history instead of writing it.[9]

The thousands upon thousands of documents still classified on the grounds of national security by the American government need to be released unredacted to show the full story of what took place at Pearl Harbor.

The one thing in closing out this book that must be reported, which adds more to the evidence that the Tanaka Memorial is a real historical document, is the story related by the famous author of the book *Call of the Wild*, Jack London. While he had been covering the Russo-Japanese War in Korea in 1905, he met a young Japanese officer called Tanaka who told him in no uncertain terms that Japan would one day attack the United States and eventually conquer the world. Once back in America, London told the newspaper that he was working for this story, but he was not allowed to write it because he had no facts to back it up. Remember, this was years before the First World War took place, and years before the Tanaka Memorial was leaked out to Young China Publishing in 1936. Again this adds to the premise that the Tanaka Memorial is legitimate. Here again historians have failed to do the proper research on this document. If history is to be researched and reported, then the truth must be told even if the heavens should fall, as a famous statesman once said.

Notes

Chapter I

1. William Mitchell, *Winged Defense 1925* (Tuscaloosa) University of Alabama Press, 2009.
2. John T. Correll, 'The Billy Mitchell Court-Martial' (Arlington) *Air Force Magazine*, August 2012, p.127.

Chapter II

1. Leon Trotsky, 'The Tanaka Memorial Review' (Moscow) *Leon Trotsky Archive Fourth International* Vol. 2 No. 5 June 1941, pp.131–135 (www.leontroskyarchive.org)
2. Robert Holden & Douglas Cervi, *The Nanking Massacre and other Japanese Atrocities Committed During the Asia-Pacific War 1931–1945* (Trenton) New Jersey Commission on Holocaust Education, 2007, p.157.
3. Giichi Tanaka, *The Tanaka Memorial* (Shanghai) Young China Publishing, 1936 (www.nationalarchives.com)
4. Carl Crow, *Japan's Dream of World Empire – The Tanaka Memorial* (New York) Harper & Brothers, 1998, pp.20–21.
5. Haruko Taya Cook & Theodore Cook, *Japan at War: An Oral History* (New York) The New Press, 1992, p.78.

Chapter III

1. Jack Young, Captain U.S.N. Retired, 'The Real Architect of Pearl Harbor' (Annapolis) *Naval Aviation Magazine*, Spring 2005, pp.1–3.
2. Joseph V. Micallef, *The First Attack: Pearl Harbor, February 7th, 1932* (Washington, D.C.) (www.military.com), 2020, pp.2–7.
3. John F. Ptak, *Pearl Harbor and the Sneak Attack of 1932* (Hendersonville), J.F. Science Books Publishing, 2019, pp.5–9.

Chapter IV

1. Elie Wiesel, *After the Darkness: Reflections of the Holocaust* (New York) Schocken Books 2002, p.16
2. Rafael Medoff, "*The Jews should keep Quiet: Franklin D. Roosevelt, Rabbi Stephen S. Wise, and the Holocaust.*" (Lincoln, Nebraska) University of Nebraska Press 2019, p.292
3. Documents: *Unit-731* (Washington, D.C.) National Archives Library of Congress (www.nationalarchives.com), 1999.

Chapter V

1. Douglas Peifer, *Presidential Crisis Decision Making Following the Sinking of the Panay* (Montgomery) United States Air War College, 5 November 2018, pp.5–27.
2. Manny Koginos, *The Panay Incident: Prelude to War* (Lafayette) Purdue University Studies, 1967, pp.129–130.
3. Document: *Secretary of State to the Ambassador in Japan (Grew) Sinking of the USS Panay Telegram, Washington December 13, 1937* (Washington, D.C.), Department of State Library of Congress National Archive, 1937.

Chapter VI

1. Philip Gavin, *Genocide in the 20th Century* (Boston) (www.historyplace.com), 2000.
2. Katsuichi Honda, *The Nanking Massacre: A Japanese Journalist Confronts Japan's National Shame* (New York), Routledge Publishing, 2015, pp.122–125.
3. Honda, p.121.
4. Document: 'Contest to Kill 100 Chinese Soldiers with Sword Extended' (Tokyo), *Nichi Nichi Shimbun* newspaper, 1937.

Chapter VIII

1. Robert Stinnett, *Day of Deceit: The Truth about FDR and Pearl Harbor* (New York), Touchstone Publishing, 2001, p.7.
2. Ibid., p.9.
3. Ibid., p.10.
4. Document: *U.S. Naval Attaché Tokyo Confidential* (Washington D.C.) RG 38 (Serial 220230) Library of Congress National Archives, 23 August 1941 (www.nationalarchives.com).

5. James O. Richardson, *On the Treadmill to Pearl Harbor: The Memoirs of Admiral James O Richardson* (Washington D.C.), Department of the Navy History Division, 1973, p.97.

Chapter IX

1. Cordell Hull, *Outline of Proposed Basis for Agreement between United States and Japan: Memo* (Washington, D.C.), Library of Congress National Archives, 26 November 1941 (www.nationalarchives.com)
2. Document: *Naval Operations* (Washington, D.C.), Library of Congress National Archives, 17 November 1941 (www.nationalarchives.com)
3. Joseph Grew, *Cablegram 125: State Department* (Washington, D.C.), Library of Congress National Archives Confidential File, 27 January 1941 PHPT (www.nationalarchives.com)

Chapter X

1. Stinnett, Robert, *Day of Deceit*, pp.71–72.

Chapter XI

1. Document: 'Japan May Strike Over Weekend' (Hilo), *Hilo Tribune Herald*, 30 November 1941.
2. Robert A. Theobald, Rear Admiral USN Retired. *The Final Secret of Pearl Harbor: The Washington Contribution to the Japanese Attack* (New York), Devin-Adair Company Publishing, 1954, p.210.
3. Document: *Message from the President to the Emperor of Japan* (Washington D.C.), Library of Congress National Archives Department of State Bulletin Vol. V No. 129 1941 (www.nationalarchives.com)
4. Document: *Joint Committee on the Investigation of the Pearl Harbor Attack* (Washington D.C.), Library of Congress National Archives, 20 June 1946 (www.nationalarchives.com)
5. Document: *Pearl Harbor* (Washington, D.C.) Vice Admiral Homer N. Wallin, Naval History Division, U.S. Government Printing Division Campaigns of the Pacific War Naval Analysis Division, 1968 (www.nationalarchives.com)
6. Document: *Cablegram MacArthur to Marshall* (Washington, D.C.) RG80, PHLO, MMRB, Library of Congress National Archives II (www.nationalarchives.com), 1941.
7. Document: *Message to Fleet Commander Pearl Harbor* (Washington, D.C.) RG38 Station US Papers MM, RB Library of Congress National Archives II (www.nationalarchives.com)

8. Document: *Climb Niitaka Yama* (Washington, D.C.) USA=SRN #115376 RG 457, 2 December 1941, Library of Congress National Archives II (www.nationalarchives.com)
9. Frederick D. Parker, *Pearl Harbor Revisited: U.S. Navy Communications Intelligence 1924–1941* (Washington, D.C.) NSA United States Center for Cryptologic History Series IV: World War II, Vol. 6, 2012.
10. Document: *Yamamoto to Fleet* (Washington D.C.), Library of Congress National Archives II, 1998 (www.nationalarchives.com)

Chapter XII

1. John Lamperti, *Remember Pearl Harbor: An Example of Pre-emptive War* (Hanover), University Press, Dartmouth, 2018.
2. Document: *James Parks Ensign USS Maryland Deck Log* (Washington, D.C.), Library of Congress National Archives, 2017 (www.nationalarchives.com)
3. Document: *F.M. Radel Ensign USS Dale Deck Log* (Washington, D.C.), Library of Congress National Archives (www.nationalarchives.com)
4. Document: *The Pearl Harbor Attack* (Pearl Harbor, Hawaii), Pearl Harbor National Memorial, 2020.
5. Mitsuo Fushida, *I Led the Attack on Pearl Harbor* (Washington, D.C.), United States Naval Intelligence Library of Congress Transcript 1952, Vol. 78/9/595, National Archives (www.nationalarchives.com)

Chapter XIII

1. Stinnett, pp.1–5.
2. Paul S. Burtness & Warren Ober, 'Provocation Against: FDR, Japan, Pearl Harbor and Entry into World War in the Pacific' (Pearl *Harbor*) *Hawaiian Journal of History*, Vol. 51, 2017.

Chapter XIV

1. Document: *English Version Hirohito/Yamamoto Dispatch Message* (Washington, D.C.) Library of Congress National Archives II SRN115371 RG457 MMRB, 1979 (www.nationalarchives.com)
2. Stinnett, p.220.
3. Document: *Letter to President Clinton from Helen Hamman* (Washington, D.C.) Red Cross Files of Don Smith Director of the War Service Red Cross 1941, Library of Congress National Archives (www.nationalarchives.com), 1995.

Chapter XV

1. Jerome T. Hagen, *War in the Pacific* (Honolulu), Hawaii Pacific University, 1996, pp. 4–7.
2. Holden & Cervi, p.158.
3. Austin Glass, *Comments on R&A/IBT Memos D 25, 26, 29, 30, 35 Dealing with Indo-China* (Washington, D.C.) Records of the Office of Strategic Services, Record group 226 RG, Entry 19, Box 175, Document XL12971 NARA National Archives.
4. James M. Scott, *Battlefield as Crime Scene: The Japanese Massacre in Manila* (Richmond), 2018 (www.historynet.com)
5. Hampton Sides, *Ghost Soldiers: The Forgotten Epic Story of World War II's Most Dramatic Mission* (New York), Doubleday Publishing, 2001, p.24.
6. John D. Lukacs, *Escape from Davao: The Forgotten Story of the most Daring Prison Break of the Pacific War* (New York), Dutton Caliber, 2010, p.321.
7. George Feifer, *The Battle of Okinawa: The Blood and the Bomb* (Guilford, Connecticut), Lyons Press, 2001, pp.422–423.
8. Ibid., p.423.
9. Carl von Clausewitz, *Principles of War* (Mineola), Dover Publications, 2003, p.68.

All photos are from the United States Library of Congress (www.nationalarchives.com)

Final Thoughts

There are many people I must thank in writing this book. First and foremost, my wife Nhan Thanh Thi Nguyen; she was so very helpful in doing my research and helping me find all of these documents in the Library of Congress/National Archives. She is my world and my co-author. Next I must thank my four PhD professors from AMU that encouraged me to write my first book, *Shiloh the 1st Day: Turning Point of the American Civil War*, and also encouraging me to write this book. They are Dr Don Sine, Dr Deborah Kidwell, Dr David Petriello and Dr Thomas Goss. Another undergrad professor who was highly motivating in my wanting to write the true history was Dr Rodderman (RIP), who told me that although 'history is a fable agreed upon,' that does not mean it is true.

Next I must mention my mother and father, Charles and Ruth Sprinkles (RIP), for telling me about their lives growing up in the 1930s and '40s and what they had to live through, which is history. Others who have supported me in my endeavors to write this book are my uncle Marvin Stanifer and my cousin Ralph Sourette. Friends that have been very supportive are Bill Ransdel, Deidra Ransdel, Josh Brock, Mike Golden, Shane Trent, Greg Richardson, Brad Hollar, Chris Slater, my wife's beautiful family, which is sister Huong Thi Nguyen, brother Cuong Huu Nguyen (R.I.P.), brother Thang Huu Nguyen, sister Bich Thi Nguyen, brother Chien Huu Nguyen, and along with my beautiful little wife Nhan Thanh Thi Nguyen I wish to thank you for all your support.

Again also to the National Archives/Library of Congress for all the information that they provided that made it possible to find these primary source documents to use in the writing of this book. With thanks also to Austin Bershear and Eric Kelley.

Bibliography

Primary Sources

Aschbrenner, Paul. *First Hand Account of the Attack on Pearl Harbor* (Johnston, Iowa) PBS Publishing, 2006 (www.iowapbs.org)

Document: *Cablegram MacArthur to Marshall* (Washington, D.C.) RG80, PHLO, MMRB, Library of Congress National Archives II (www.nationalarchives.com), 1941.

Document: *Climb Niitaka Yama* (Washington, D.C.) USA=SRN #115376 RG 457 2 December 1941, Library of Congress National Archives II (www.nationalarchives.com)

Cook, Haruko T. & Theodore F. Cook. *Japan at War: An Oral History* (New York, New York) The New Press, 1992.

Grew, Joseph. *Cablegram 125: State Department* (Washington, D.C.) Library of Congress National Archives Confidential File January 27, 1941 PHPT (www.nationalarchives.com)

Document: 'Contest to Kill 100 Chinese Soldiers with Sword Extended' (Tokyo, Japan) *Nichi Nichi Shimbun* newspaper, 1937.

Fushida, Mitsuo, *I Led the Attack on Pearl Harbor* (Washington, D.C.) United States Naval Intelligence Library of Congress Transcript 1952 Volume 78/9/595 National Archives (www.nationalarchives.com)

Document: *English Version Hirohito/Yamamoto Dispatch Message* (Washington, D.C.) Library of Congress National Archives II SRN115371 RG457 MMRB, 1979 (www.nationalarchives.com)

Glass, Austin, *Comments on R&A/IBT Memos D_25, 26, 29, 30, 35 Dealing with Indo-China* (Washington, D.C.) Records of the Office of Strategic Services, Record group 226 RG, Entry 19, Box 175, Document XL12971 NARA National Archives.

Hull, Cordell, *Outline of Proposed Basis for Agreement between United States and Japan: Memo* (Washington, D.C.) Library of Congress National Archives, 26 November 1941 (www.nationalarchives.com)

Document: *Japan May Strike Over Weekend* (Hilo, Hawaii) *Hilo Tribune Herald*, 30 November 1941.

Document: *Joint Committee on the Investigation of the Pearl Harbor Attack* (Washington D.C.) Library of Congress National Archives, 20 June 1946 (www.nationalarchives.com)

Document: *Letter to President Clinton from Helen Hamman* (Washington, D.C.) Red Cross Files of Don Smith Director of the War Service Red Cross 1941 Library of Congress National Archives (www.nationalarchives.com), 1995.

Kajimoto, Masato. *Japanese Soldiers Diaries and Interviews of the Nanking Massacre* (Tokyo, Japan) (www.thenankingmassacre.org), 2000.

Document: *Message to Fleet Commander Pearl Harbor* (Washington, D.C.) RG38 Station US Papers MM, RB Library of Congress National Archives II (www.nationalarchives.com)

Document: *Message from the President to the Emperor of Japan* (Washington D.C.) Library of Congress National Archives Department of State Bulletin Volume V No.1 29 1941 (www.nationalarchives.com)

Document: *Naval Operations* (Washington, D.C.) Library of Congress National Archives, 27 November 1941 (www.nationalarchives.com)

Document: *James Parks Ensign USS Maryland Deck Log* (Washington, D.C.) Library of Congress National Archives 2017 (www.nationalarchives.com)

Document: *Pearl Harbor* (Washington, D.C.) Vice Admiral Homer N. Wallin, Naval History Division, U.S. Government Printing Division Campaigns of the Pacific War Naval Analysis Division 1968 (www.nationalarchives.com)

Document: *The Pearl Harbor Attack* (Pearl Harbor, Hawaii) Pearl Harbor National Memorial, 2020.

Document: *F.M. Radel Ensign USS Dale Deck Log* (Washington, D.C.) Library of Congress National Archives (www.nationalarchives.com)

Document: *Secretary of State to the Ambassador in Japan (Grew) Sinking of the USS Panay Telegram, Washington December 13, 1937* (Washington, D.C.) Department of State Library of Congress National Archive 1937 (www.nationalarchives.com)

Tanaka, Giichi. *The Tanaka Memorial* (Shanghai, China) Young China Publishing, 1936 (www.nationalarchives.com)

Documents: *Unit-731* (Washington, D.C.) National Archives Library of Congress (www.nationalarchives.com), 1999.

Document: *U.S. Naval Attaché Tokyo Confidential* (Washington D.C.) RG 38 (Serial 220230) Library of Congress National Archives, 23 August 1941 (www.nationalarchives.com)

Document: *United States Note to Japan November 26, 1941* (Washington, D.C.) Library of Congress National Archives Department of States Bulletin Volume 5 No. 129, 13 December 1941 (www.nationalarchives.com)

Document: *Yamamoto to Fleet* (Washington D.C.) Library of Congress National Archives II 1998 (www.nationalarchives.com)

Secondary Sources

Brandon, Mark, *Japan's War and the United States Failure with Japanese War Crimes* (London, England) (www.pacificwar.org.au), 2018.

Burtness, Paul S. & Warren Ober, 'Provocation Against: FDR, Japan, Pearl Harbor and Entry into World War in the Pacific' (Pearl Harbor, Hawaii) *Hawaiian Journal of History*, Volume 51, 2017.

Chang, Iris, *The Rape of Nanking: The Forgotten Holocaust of World War II* (New York, New York) Basic Books, 1997.

Clausewitz, Carl von, *The Principles of War* (Mineola, New York) Dover Publications, 2003.

Correll, John T., 'The Billy Mitchell Court-Martial' (Arlington, Virginia) *Air Force Magazine*, August 2012.

Cressman, Robert, *Pearl Harbor Attack: Dec 7, 1941* (Washington, D.C.) Navy History and Heritage Command (www.history.navy.mil)

Crow, Carl, *Japan's Dream of World Empire-The Tanaka Memorial* (New York, New York) Harper & Brothers, 1998.

Feifer, George, *The Battle of Okinawa: The Blood and the Bomb* (Guilford, Connecticut) Lyons Press, 2001.

Gavin, Philip, *Genocide in the 20th Century* (Boston, Massachusetts) (www.historyplace.com), 2000.

Ghose, Ishani, *FBI had Information about Pearl Harbor Attack 4 Months before Japanese Offensive* (Karnataka, India) 28 March 2019 (www.meaww.com)

Haddick, Rick, *This Week at War: Strategic Error* (McLean, Virginia) Small Wars Journals (www.smallwarjournal.com), 2012.

Hagen, Jerome T., *War in the Pacific* (Honolulu, Hawaii), Hawaii Pacific University, 1996.

Heilbrunn, Jacob, *Did Navy Code Breakers Know Japan was Going to Strike Pearl Harbor* (Washington, D.C.), 21 March 2020 (www.nationalinterest.org)

Holden, Robert & Douglas Cervi, *The Nanking Massacre and other Japanese Atrocities Committed During the Asia-Pacific War 1931–1945* (Trenton, New Jersey) New Jersey Commission on Holocaust Education, 2007.

Honda, Katsuichi, *The Nanking Massacre: A Japanese Journalist Confronts Japans National Shame* (New York, New York) Routledge Publishing, 2015.

Kahn, David, 'Attack on Pearl Harbor: Why we Were not Warned' (Leesburg, Virginia) *World War II Magazine*, 2001.

Klein, Christopher, *The Midget Sub that Beat the Planes to Pearl Harbor* (Richmond, Virginia) 6 December 2019 (www.history.com)
Koginos, Manny, *The Panay Incident: Prelude to War* (Lafayette, Indiana) Purdue University Studies, 1967.
Kristof, Nicholas D., 'Un-Masking Horror-A Special Report: Japan's Confronting Gruesome War Atrocity' (New York, New York) *New York Times*, 17 March 1995.
Lamperti, John, *Remember Pearl Harbor: An Example of Pre-emptive War* (Hanover, New Hampshire) University Press Dartmouth, 2018.
Lukacs, John D., *Escape from Davao: The Forgotten Story of the most Daring Prison Break of the Pacific War* (New York, New York) Dutton Caliber, 2010.
Lyons, Chuck, *Attack on U.S.S. Panay* (Richmond, Virginia) Warfare History Network (www.warfarehistorynetwork.com), 17 January 2019.
Malm, Sara, 'The Horrors of Japan's WWII Human Experiments Unit: Disturbing Reports of how Chinese Civilians and Allied P.O.W.s were Dissected Alive and Infected with the Plague' (London, England) *Daily Mail News*, May 2018.
McDaniel, Christopher, *Documents Reveal FDR May Have Known About Pearl Harbor Attack* (New York, New York) MIC Network Company, 2012 (www.mic.com)
Micallef, Joseph V., *The First Attack: Pearl Harbor, February 7th, 1932* (Washington, D.C) (www.military.com), 2020.
Mitchell, William, *Winged Defense 1925* (Tuscaloosa, Alabama) University of Alabama Press, 2009.
Parker, Frederick D., *Pearl Harbor Revisited: U.S. Navy Communications Intelligence 1924–1941* (Washington, D.C.) NSA United States Center for Crypto logic History Series IV: World War II Volume 6, 2012.
Peifer, Douglas, *Presidential Crisis Decision Making Following the Sinking of the Panay* (Montgomery, Alabama) United States Air War College, 5 November 2018.
Ptak, John F., *Pearl Harbor and the Sneak Attack of 1932* (Hendersonville, North Carolina) J.F. Science Books Publishing, 2019.
Richardson, James O., *On the Treadmill to Pearl Harbor: The Memoirs of Admiral James O Richardson* (Washington D.C.) Department of the Navy History Division, 1973.
Rothman, Lily, 'The Pearl Harbor Mystery that Still Makes People Wonder' (New York, New York) *Time Magazine*, 2016.
Scott, James M., *Battlefield as Crime Scene: The Japanese Massacre in Manila* (Richmond, Virginia), 2018 (www.historynet.com)
Sides, Hampton, *Ghost Soldiers: The Forgotten Epic Story of World War II most Dramatic Mission* (New York, New York) Doubleday Publishing, 2001.

Silva, Mallary, *Conspiracy: Did FDR Deceive American People in a Push for War* (Boston, Massachusetts) Inquires Journal 2010 Volume 2 No. 1 (www.inquiriesjournal.com)

Staff Writer, *Billy Mitchell Prophecy* (Rockville, Maryland) American Heritage Volume 13 Issue 2, 1962 (www.americanheritage.com)

Steely, Shipper, *Pearl Harbor Countdown: The Biography of Admiral James O. Richardson* (Gretna, Louisiana) Pelican Press, 2008.

Stinnett, Robert, *Day of Deceit: The Truth about FDR and Pearl Harbor* (New York, New York) Touchstone Publishing, 2001.

Theobald, Robert A., Rear Admiral USN Retired, *The Final Secret of Pearl Harbor: The Washington Contribution to the Japanese Attack* (New York, New York) Devin-Adair Company Publishing, 1954.

Trotsky, Leon, *The Tanaka Memorial Review* (Moscow, Russia) Leon Trotsky Archive Fourth International Volume 2 No. 5 June 1941 (www.leontroskyarchive.org)

Weinberg, Gerhard L., *Germany Hitler & World War II* (New York, New York) University of Cambridge Press, 1995.

Young, Jack Captain U.S.N. Retired, 'The Real Architect of Pearl Harbor' (Annapolis, Maryland) *Naval Aviation Magazine*, Spring 2005.

About the Authors

Charles Sprinkles and his co-author and wife Nhan Thanh Thi Nguyen, live in Lexington, Kentucky, where he teaches online at a southern university. This is his second book, his first was *Shiloh The 1st Day: Turning Point of the American Civil War*, which came out in 2018. Charles has a double masters degree in Military History and Global History from the American Military University. He has served over twenty years as a United States Army Infantry Reserve Officer. Charles also belongs to the Historical Studies Honor Society and is a member of the Knights Templar and Shriner organisation. His wife is from Haiphong, Vietnam, and their son, Albert Van Doan, is in the Canadian Army and lives in Canada.